The
Anatomy of
Wake-Up Calls

Volume 2

The
Anatomy of
Wake-Up Calls

Volume 2

Psychology of Survival

Dr. Feridoun Shawn Shahmoradian

THE ANATOMY OF WAKE-UP CALLS VOLUME 2
PSYCHOLOGY OF SURVIVAL

iUniverse books may be ordered through booksellers or by contacting:

iUniverse
1663 Liberty Drive
Bloomington, IN 47403
www.iuniverse.com
1-800-Authors (1-800-288-4677)

ISBN: 978-1-5320-0500-8 (sc)
ISBN: 978-1-5320-0501-5 (e)

Library of Congress Control Number: 2015917037

Print information available on the last page.

iUniverse rev. date: 08/18/2016

Table of Contents

Foreword

This groundbreaking collection of essays delves into essential issues of our time in need of urgent attention. Dynamic solutions are sought to untangle fact from fiction, as the puzzling questions surrounding these issues have led humanity to react impetuously, resulting in the destabilization of social security and a web of cultural, social, financial, psychological and philosophical uncertainties. The author presents a host of insightful and practical remedies, ushering readers toward the proverbial light at the end of tunnel, where the veil of ambiguities is lifted. These truths are reserved only for inquisitive souls in search of enlightenment, with intent to accentuate and honor the sacred properties of man within whom the image of God resides and with impetus to fuel the asphyxiation of the essence of evil.

We should strive for the alliance of mankind and geometric progression toward a global common good. The quality of wisdom and understanding depends on the quality and the characteristics of the undertaker when challenging the life-threatening problems facing humanity. Society must comprehend that we are not commodities; we are part a of cosmic spirit with a conscious soul designed so delicately that emotion can pierce into the very core of our beings; when one is under the spell of emotion and hypnotized by one's feelings, sometimes no amount of logic or intellect can stop one from doing the unthinkable—call it creation, evolution, or call it as you please. We are made to love and belong. When one becomes deprived of love and caring and does not fit in, he or she tends to rebel and exercise the motives of the lower self through ugly and depraved behavior. The result of this phenomenon can be manifested in horrific shapes and abhorrent forms that can put the most vicious animal to shame. Often deceived by our own minds, we are even more vulnerable to doing wrong when an atmosphere to fluster people's feelings and pollute the human psyche is adeptly designed and creatively manipulated behind the curtain.

It is crucial to understand that our strength is in numbers. A war of attrition depends significantly on the power of the vote, where ominous tactics can be foiled and the exultant dance of victory can be triggered through oneness. Together, we can stubbornly deploy an epic journey to overcome these arduous challenges promulgated by those in power, whose interests represent a detriment to society. Such action can often evolve into a marathon ascent, preventing the broods of evil from doing wrong and allowing people to find sanctuary from the clutches of wickedness. This is not a plot to facilitate revolutionary violence or to lambaste others' behavior, ending in bloodshed, but rather a savvy camaraderie to exercise collective bargaining, power of reasoning, integrity, accountability and the potency of rational dialogue to save precious human lives. Immanuel Kent's *Theory of Religion* says this about radical evil: "It's less about a group of people, but about the evil within us all." I would like to add to this by saying:

> *It is about the sublime madness within all of us which needs to be tamed. Deprivation of empathy and wisdom can make anyone a potential threat; cruel and indignant actions cannot have a conscience, despite possessing the physical appearance of one, nor identify with any other portion of a human being's narrative. Unless we become harmonized with our good natures and everyone acts from his or her higher self (where fear and lack of awareness are truly questioned), no hope for peace and social tranquility is probable. Such action is not against the preservation of the moral imperative of justice, but is additionally fueled by the power of intellect and rational thinking. Ratiocination should be prioritized in moments of extremity, in contrast to the overwhelming power of insanity that dictates the exertion of brute force to divert the legitimate anger of the powerless.*

Envisage your trust in God, believe in yourself, believe in compassion, and believe in a humanity devoid of the bitter fruit of demagoguery, inundated with anger and empty rhetoric. Manipulative behavior often serves the interest of the insanely ambitious and prank-minded individual, as well as capricious exuberant groups. Let's blast the borders and call for one government, one nation under God; let's make friends, shun avarice, be humble, help others, and let's scream the loudest and dance the hardest to triumph over the ignorance within us to assert that "life is meant to be good." Know that the joy and ecstasy of living is not an illusion, but an actual taste of intense spiritual feelings delivered through the vehicle of a magnificent human neurological system that can manifest elation beyond imagination. This gift can only work to the fullest, however, if a blithe and constructive atmosphere is made available to experience these heavenly human sensations.

We should honor those exemplifying absolute serenity and an undisturbed meditative state of mind during a near death experience. Many individuals independently claim that they were so deeply relaxed and clear-minded while experiencing "tunnel vision" and an extremely illuminating light, and were solaced by the fact that they seemed they knew the answers to everything. Scientifically this makes sense because brain memory is at its peak while one is in a trancelike state. The experience is one of utter tranquility of mind with no thought interferences. This valuable lesson learned should be applied to the everyday blizzard of manufactured anxieties associated with a stressful lifestyle, as well as to the frequent malicious misdeeds purposely orchestrated to act as stumbling blocks within our society. The resulting apprehension denies so many the power of dynamic thinking and is impervious to the spirit of gaiety, depriving mankind from making magic on Earth to rival the heavens above.

Essay 1
Dreams and the REM State of Mind

Dreams occur in the state known as "REM sleep." REM stands for *rapid eye movement*, where eye movements are fast and directed to various sides—where our eyes move quickly in many directions. Reaching this state is a result of a relaxed state of mind, where there is total serenity. During REM, the brain experiences a complete stillness, much like a deep meditative state. Perhaps it feels odd to say that at this stage, when deep sleep takes over and we unconsciously breathe deeply, we are as relaxed as a baby.

During the REM state, our mind can often go beyond our human limitations. In our dreams, for example, we are able to fly and can communicate with our deceased loved ones as if they are still with us. We can break into other dimensions and beyond known boundaries when the mind is clear and not disturbed with daily pressures—when we are not stressed or perhaps influenced by fear, anxiety, or other agitating states. We are not able to perform or reference such tasks when we are conscious and awake, as life's stressors tend to convolute, distract, impede, and otherwise engage our brains with looking for solutions to daily obstacles; this limits and prevents us from performing dynamic maneuvers. Because of anxiety, fear, pain, and suffering and other malice, we are essentially blocked from the ability to reach our higher goals.

It is also believed that before reaching a REM state of sleep, one goes through three stages of "non-REM" sleep, which roughly last from five to twenty minutes each. Then, REM sleep begins and can last from ten minutes to one hour; this is when our brain is believed to activate intense dreams. Normally REM sleep occurs about ninety-five minutes to two hours after we fall asleep; this includes our passing through the three stages of non-REM sleep before entering REM sleep.

In the first stage of sleep it is easy to wake up; we are barely asleep. Then, in the second stage of sleep, known also as "light sleep," everything slows down, including body temperature and heart rate, as we head toward a deep sleep. In the third stage of sleep—when we are about to enter into REM sleep—if we were to be disturbed, we would be disoriented and confused for a little while before recovering. Also in this third phase many beneficial things happen, including our body's ability to repair itself: creating bone, growing new tissues and muscle, and strengthening our immune system to fight diseases.

H.F Hedge said, "Dream is an act of pure imagination, a behest in all men with a creative power, which if it were available in waking, would make everyman a Dante or Shakespeare." I believe the hypotheses of string theory and quantum physics, which acknowledge that perhaps one day the ability to access other dimensions can happen, enabling man to reach beyond the limited space and time we can presently experience. One day this ability will open up into an enormous and miraculous life discovery. This has a lot to do with the soaring of human imagination and is a must-believe prophecy. Our mind must be completely calm and unfettered with distress, not enslaved with uneasiness. With training we shall learn that our minds can become revolutionized and can become ready to switch into "REM" mode at will. If this is the case, then as Henri Amiel explains, "Dreams are excursions into the limbo of things, a semi deliverance from the human prison."

We should persist in moving further and further away from our current chaotic and distressful life style, which is presently postponing a real breakthrough in freeing our mind from this inhibited domain and restraining thought process. Scientists say that people who say they never dream simply do not remember their dreams. A study of patients with REM disorder suggests that we all dream. I also believe our dreams are a mechanism that acts like a safety valve on a pressure cooker, meaning that they serve to release some of the daily pressures already built up within us. Occasionally dreams replay some of our deepest thoughts encapsulated in our subconscious mind, screaming and impatiently waiting for a way out; this does not exclude human sexual fantasies.

French scientist Michel Jouvet construed the idea of computer metaphor, which spurred scientists to regard REM sleep in the fetus and the newborn as the time when the software of our brain is programmed. It is believed that during REM sleep, the brain is disconnected from any sensory input from the external world by the restriction of major muscles, known by scientists as anti- gravity muscles, which are all paralyzed during REM sleep. It was Jouvet's experimentation that created some of the essential building blocks for understanding the function of the REM state. It was also Jouvet who made the restriction of anti-gravity muscles during REM sleep known. He said that REM sleep, which he referred to as paradoxical sleep, might play the role of programming the central nervous system to maintain or organize instinctive actions.

The REM state is the mechanism that links us with reality; it systematically runs in the background, searching out and scanning at lightning speed the codes required to match metaphorically to whatever makes sense in the environment, therefore creating our perception of reality. It creates reality-oriented situations, forming the rudimentary templates that are the basis of meaning. This is noticed when people retrieve memories that invoke strong emotions; rapid eye movements happen even when our eyes are open. This is true when we dream and is also a fact when we daydream. It has been witnessed that when people go into a deep state of concentration (<u>trance</u>) and potent instincts are awakened, hallucinations and the <u>hearing of voices may result</u>.

When we are in the dream state, and evidently when REM is at the height of its activity —our sensory information is abundant and yet shut off from the reality of outside world—the templates looking for completion scan the brain and make metaphorical images from memory. Our mind holds these images and while we are dreaming, they become the reality rendered into consciousness. This reality in our dreams is profoundly explicit and richer than in our waking reality. Each particular allegorical (symbolic) dream image can hold multiple levels of meanings. Dreams mobilize emotional awakening, and do so within several channels of arousal with the same image at the same time. Meditation is the closest thing to deep sleep, where a veteran meditator—perhaps a Buddhist monk or practitioner of Sufism—can go beyond the mind and into what is known as trance. Here the meditator enters into absolute silence, acquiring the ability to experience other realms of being, resulting in a complete unawareness of his surroundings.

Our waking reality is very different. It is dramatically scaled down, because it is infiltrated with other mind-occupying agendas; this disturbs the potential for total focus and hence total serenity and clarity of mind are virtually impossible in our daily lives. However, if we constantly noticed multiple levels of meaning in everything at the same time, we wouldn't be able to make sense of, or operate within, our environment. Our mental state and psyche would become confused and perhaps in disarray, leading to psychotic behavior and an inability to take care of our responsibilities and daily chores. To deal with this problem, the neo-cortex of the brain (the rational part of our awaked mind) inhibits multi-meaning.

That is exactly why we must recall our dreams immediately after we are awakened to the reality of our world. After a short span of time, within the interval of couple of minutes or a little longer, we become completely detached from the details of our dreams and cannot remember exactly what transpired. We are now back into our regular life routine, resuming the reality of our being. This entire scenario materializes because our conscious mind kicks into gear, activating our thought processes and awareness of our daily problems, i.e.: what needs to be done. Often we become entangled within a web of uncertainties trying to determine what is next on our to-do list, trying to find answers to the host of complexities facing us, and thus instantly clouding our very memory, forcing it to incompletely remember our dreams. This is unfortunate, as Sigmund Freud noted: "Dreams are often most profound when they seem the craziest."

Essay 2

Individualism or a Yoke?

We are living in a very dangerous time, in fact so perilous that the single push of a button can literally kill hundreds of millions of innocent people. Humanity is faced with serious problems, the most fundamental of which is losing sight of our human dignity and virtues, and becoming complacent about our integrity to behold the truth and what is right. Self-interest is unleashed where human decency is lost, and the love of accumulating wealth and power has blinded many to do the unspeakable. There is no balance left in capitalism, since fair competition has turned into a monopoly aimed at crushing other competitors with no remorse. Self-interest has turned into plundering, becoming a way of life for the powerful—a filthy habit leading to addiction, making monsters out of corporate capitalists and the public enemies of our time.

Social movements aimed at saving humanity, not based on building empires, can shift the balance of power. Such movements create fundamental and dynamic changes because policies are not made based on class priorities but on flowing together in the name of justice and peace, and in the name social safety. In this environment, delusional geniuses and perpetrators of hatred cannot sit atop the material world, causing havoc and total destruction with the stroke of a pen, fueled by insecurity, self-absorption, greed, fear, and anxiety.

Movements must be based upon vision and dreams, on reason and collective wisdom, and where politics and social movements are not fettered with chains of ignorance and selfishness. Our focus must be where human values are manifested to avoid the potential for nuclear war, in the redistribution of wealth, in saving the planet, and in halting terrorism. Pragmatic policies must truly be made for the collective security, where balance is preserved and therefore neither capitalism nor socialism can take charge of our lives for the worse, but instead seek other available alternatives which are not meant to knock everyone out like a game of chess where the powerful corporate capitalists or the communist commissars rule the world at the expense of the masses.

Unless we change ourselves, we cannot change the world and the mess we are in; a cultural revolution is needed to enlighten people. Consider our goal to be similar to the completion of a jigsaw puzzle. Unlike chess, which is black and white, with a target of exterminating others – in a jigsaw puzzle there are whole range of colors at work. The objective of a jigsaw puzzle is not to win, but to fit all the pieces together with calculated patience. The excruciating pain and suffering that most of humanity is experiencing must be remedied in the name of good conscience and through the energy of the cosmic Mother. This remedy should be administered through compassion, through the pursuit of our hopes and dreams, through collective wisdom, intelligence, and awakened spirit. Within this spirit we identify our commonalities and heal our differences peacefully. We heal through love for each other, by abandoning desolate and inhumane behaviors, and by learning to "live and let live," as equals—where the essence of virtue is magnified and truly practiced in the name of God and his children.

We cannot just respond casually to urgent matters confronting the very existence of humanity and the planet Earth we live on. We need not to respond with centrifugal force toward the vital issues that are threatening all of humanity by the few individuals completely impervious to the decency of reason and meaningful living. It seems that greed, pride, and crushing ambitions have altered their brains to accept that so much wrongdoing is inevitable and acceptable for humankind. Times have changed. Many of our laws are outdated and not practical, and we have reached an era of globalism, which certainly demands new cultural and socioeconomic policies. Such policies have a moral obligation to adequately respond to the contemporary and vital demands of a global nation under one God and one government. International military complexes, with their potential hazards of atomic, biological and chemical warfare and international terrorism are definitely a serious threat to the entire world. Socrates, the Greek philosopher, believed that nobody willingly chooses to do wrong. He maintained that doing wrong always harms the wrongdoer and that nobody seeks to bring harm upon themselves. In this view, all wrongdoing is the result of ignorance. This means that it is impossible for a human being to willingly do wrong because their instinct for self-preservation prevents them from doing so.

This is an extraordinary statement that strikes disbelief in many people, going all the way back to Aristotle. It seems contrary to experience that nobody knowingly does wrong. Perhaps you have personally witnessed examples of people who did wrong and seemed to know full well that their behavior was wrong. I propose that this belief of Socrates is true in a clear and simple way. It is true that people can choose to do things they know other people think are wrong. It is even true that people can choose to do things that they believe are wrong for others while trying to benefit themselves. However, people do not choose to do things that they perceive in the moment of decision to be harmful to themselves. Humans have a powerful instinct to benefit themselves. Even when there is an obvious inherent self-harm in the action, people can do wrong and cause harm while their goal is to seek the good they believe carries benefit to them. Our objective knowledge is often subordinate to the power of our intuitive personal self-understanding. It is our personal intuition combined with a sense of our own well-being that spurs our choice to do, or have a compulsion to do, a particular wrong even when that wrongdoing will obviously harm us. And I say that is why collective wisdom and decision-making is a must; decisive majority voting should prevent destruction and group annihilation by an ignorant individual where self-interest has taken over his or her savviness of mind, thus completely blocking rational thinking.

There are so many variables that play a decisive role in keeping us apart and weary of each other. The workings of our society are inflated with fiction and lies in order to stir up trouble for the benefit of the few, based on a system of "divide and conquer." People are figuratively blindfold and led to deceitful participation in horrifying crimes such as genocide, mass murder, and the operation of institutionalized brothel houses, where many innocent children are the product of rape and the victims of a system that has prioritized profit over the fate of the people. Organized crimes such as human trafficking and child molestation are committed in the name of money, sex and violence; such activities, as well as the malevolent treatment of helpless women, and are subtly encouraged. Hence, the system makes people into nonsocial beings, and turns us against each other for its own self- gratification.

I need to reiterate that one voice is not enough to stop these and hundreds of other sickening behaviors. Collectively, we can pierce through the socioeconomic malfeasance and moral ills of our time, surgically removing these malignant tumors from the very body of the global financial system. If we do not, they will metastasize and destroy the entire body. So many serious and dysfunctional agendas currently endanger planet Earth and her inhabitants. The fact is that we have been ideologically molded to believe that this is the way life works, as they have made sociopaths out of many individuals, perpetuating the most vicious crimes against others with no remorse. The corporate oligarchy is quite potent and serves as an effective catalyst, instrumental in disemboweling the very system that capitalism is made of. In the meantime, people need to alter their thought processes and behaviors so that everyone can live in peace, collectively utilizing the conscious means available to humanity to be optimistic and affluent. In this case, "affluent" refers not to the accumulation of wealth by the few, but rather in terms of the many in living a decent life and sustaining a bright future. Both a lapse in reasoning and our complacency toward the less fortunate are contributing to the asphyxiation of millions, who are unable to survive these holocaust-like actions imposed on humanity by the few.

Why is it that we are so numb to the real reasons behind the destruction and unhappiness caused by a few financial bullies? What is it that holds us back from understanding that we all belong to the human race? Gloom and disparity should not prevail and will only serve to ruin our tranquility and hopes for a better life; we must learn to avoid these daily-near death experiences. Why should the hypocrisy in what is said and done not be decisively exposed and condemned? Such exposure could potentially precipitate a positive and practical shift, saving billions of innocent souls. Why it is that no one cares? How this apathy is fueled to such an extent that moral depravity and abjectness cannot be mended? Has humanity been stricken with dementia, cognitively deteriorating and disoriented from what is actually happening around us? What is this one thing called individualism that most humans are obsessed with, yet despite their obsession, they do not realize the current catastrophe? Why is it that some act featherheaded, and do not see this self-centeredness that has gravitated to the gentry who holds almost all the resources and power? What has kept the rest fighting for bones while these tycoons and aristocrats live beyond affluence, blinded with selfishness and leaving others with the constant anxiety of not knowing whether they will have crumbs left on their table to feed their families or not? There are no constructive plans or reliable solutions offered to accommodate them even with the most basic subsistence, therefore they are left to await their own destruction. Hillary Clinton once said, "Many of you are well enough off that the tax cut may have helped you. We are saying that for America to get back on track, we are probably going to cut that short and not give it to you. We are going to take things away from you on behalf of the common good." Why is it that we are so brainwashed into believing their weasel-like excuses about the economy and how the financial world should maneuver? They never address the real causes of our demise, or the actual underlying reasons and motives behind them. It is obvious that no dynamic solution will be reached unless we act collectively to seek a viable solution and act in concert, to truly act through the concept that "when one is hurt, all are hurt."

Unfettered and unrestrained capitalism will exploit everyone and everything in its path until society is bled dry and falls into literal collapse. Our thought processes regarding infrastructure must be committed to belief in our fellow human beings regardless of race, nationality, rank and class, religion, gender, or any another dividing factor. We should respect the rule of law that is not biased and discriminatory towards anyone, either rich or poor, a rule of law that does not believe in booking and imprisoning the deprived and the hungry, knowing they are the victims of a broken monetary system. The hope for meaningful democracy will become alive again only if people are enlightened to ask "why?" with regard to police militarism against the most vulnerable and the poor, against the minorities, the migrants, the liberals, against women, immigrants, and the destitute.

We need to dismantle the current structure of systematic oppression against the youth through mass incarceration as we simultaneously force them to becoming the victims of an abusive financial system. The so-called correctional environment is incentivized to extort taxpayers' money and unjustly punish many in the name of law; corporate tyranny has even invaded our justice system—supposedly the most sacred entity under which the helpless and harassed must take refuge. Human moral imperative rightly dictates that since the powerless are infused with truth-seeking in justice and human rights, they can overwhelmingly overcome the evils of our time, no matter how potent of a force they are. This can only occur, however, if we fraternize and flock together against the trampling of people's rights to freedom and democracy. This whole system and the government representing it need to acutely honor what the constitution and the Bill of Rights clearly state: government by the people, of the people, and for the people. That is what a true republic should be—not a government by the corporate, of the corporate and for the corporate. Inverted totalitarianism is creeping towards a Coup D'état, stripping people from their God-given rights and welfare, while keeping the masses of people apart so that collective movements are seen as rebellious. People's passion and desperate ways of life have left them no choice but to fight back for survival; even the crumbs left on the table are desperately fought for.

The privileged one percent are leveraged with corporate power and influence, yet are blinded to the desperate lifestyles of those depleted of social ranking and wealth— those who are constantly in fear of making it to the next day due to the impact of constant anxiety in not being able to afford basic subsistence and how to pay the ever-growing bills and expenses. While billions of dollars are wasted on industrial militarism for no good reason, and millions of dollars are given away to CEOs and top executives of these irresponsible corporations, the whole nation has to fight over a two or three dollar increase in minimum wage; people who can barely survive are further exploited just to stay alive. These monstrous actions can only soften the way for a bloody and violent revolution. Many innocent lives will be endangered, and those with the same trend of thought as their predecessors who helped to build capitalism will be destroyed seeking devolution to make a new progressive system possible. There are already prevalent acts of faith rising and resisting this uncivilized way of life. Billions around the globe are questioning corporate capitalism's outrageous behaviors that deny inhabitants their right to live. Corporate capitalists hold all the resources, and are ruining the entire planet Earth and its ecosystem for the majority, literally robbing them from exercising their happiness and livelihood. These blatant atrocities toward the indigent and the oppressed should alert us all to stand for the globally oppressed. Be aware of what our heavenly teacher and father Jesus of Nazareth said while being nailed to the cross by the ignorant Romans soldiers of evil: "forgive them father, as they do not know what they are doing."

Yes, we must collaborate in the exchange of knowledge and insightful information, with the goal of working together to stop catastrophes about to happen and to fight against social injustice, environmental racism, and other life-threatening issues. Mankind must be enabled to effectively resolve serious dilemmas facing us all through collective wisdom, since it is difficult for the average man to see all the hidden agendas, to discern where the system's covert exploitations are, and to ascertain how the rule of law is bent to favor corporate capitalists. This whole economic system is designed to be classified, and perhaps it should be, since all sorts of vocations are needed to maintain the balance in productivity and wealth of a nation. In the meantime we need to be vigilant of a rigged financial system that has affected the common man for the worse, and where voting rights are mysteriously being curbed. The wealthy are buying off representatives who receive millions of dollars in financial support from powerful lobbyists. This is in turn made lawful through deceitful attorneys, who take advantage of loopholes and improvise inhumane tactics to tilt the balance in favor of their breadwinners, and against the public.

William Comer said, "We are living in a sick society filled with people who would not directly steal from their neighbors, but who are willing to demand the government do it for them." It is further fair to say that workers are elated to have a job, yet are barely able to manage their own basic subsistence, being stuck in a substandard life. They either do not know, or do not care about being underpaid or about the piracy of their actual wages by their employers. It should be clear that greed and individualism can become fertile where vigilance and supervision fall short. Practicing individualism is manufactured, and not in accord with human nature, which holds that we are meant to be group animals.

We should then peacefully contest and attest to this evil of manipulation, and believe in each other and all of humanity, not only self, if we are to survive and become meaningful in pursuing the true purpose in our lives.

We can be enticed to sell out and be bought, singled out and motivated by some fringe benefits offered. When we act as individuals, all sorts of ruses can occur because when we are conditioned to act in self-interest, the probability of giving into deceptive practices and betrayals rises. This only makes us the real victims of the cruel misconduct of the super-rich. Fredrick Douglas said, "Where justice is denied, where poverty is enforced, where ignorance prevails, and where any one class is made to feel that society is an organized conspiracy to oppress, rob, and degrade them, neither person, nor property will be safe."

When spurred by greed we are most likely to become an instrument of pain and suffering for others. When we are extremely stratified, with only a few of us being well off, then expect a culture of superiority complexes to become prevalent. When we believe in promoting self by any means and are not considerate of others, bad things can happen. Machiavelli said, "Cunning, deceit, duplicities, bad faith, deception and other culprits are all permissible when contesting." He also clarified that "the end does justify the means." What he professed is truly fertile ground for the seed of hatred and animosity in cutthroat societies.

It seems this is exactly what the corporate capitalists are doing, even to their own companies. Fair competition is supposed to be the essence of capitalism and a free enterprise system, while monopolies shun just and fair competition. Franklin D. Roosevelt said, "We are trying to construct a more inclusive society. We are going to make a country in which no one is left out." The solution is to find a moderate ground that is not dictatorial (which could kick us in the rear end if given a chance), and where liberty, democracy and human rights, along with justice and peace, can truly prevail. This new ground must give people a chance to live outside of extreme poverty or deprivation, and discourage the practice of only a few possessing astronomical digits of wealth and power, since these few do not know what to do with it. The truth is that no amount of wealth can make us happy when devoted only to our own agenda, pursuing and reaching our own objectives at any cost, and acting like others do not matter. Making each person count and helping them have a voice with which to pursue their happiness and dreams will no doubt collectively resonate with people's happiness and sense of hope for better living in the name of peace. For a truly free and democratic world to exist, there would be no exploitation of any kind to fetter humanity.

Why is it that we feel so alone even when surrounded by many? Are we really happier than before, even with so much technology and progress? We can see obnoxious behaviors and negative energy everywhere; we are numb to the reality of our surroundings. It is as if everyone is in a trance, not knowing what should actually take priority in our lives other than petty interest and pride. This has a domino effect, encouraging bad mannerisms, conducive to self-interest, and fostering egotism in all that we do. Hillary Clinton once said, "We must stop thinking of the individual and start thinking what is best for society."

Could it be that in not caring, in our denials and indifference, we are perhaps erecting a self-defense mechanism against death? Our minds are perhaps molded by the popular rhetoric that tells us that "life is too short," that we need to max out our pleasure and possess a hedonistic attitude no matter the cost. Or is it just pure and simple ignorance as we commit the most atrocious, abominable, and horrifying crimes against the helpless, thinking they will go unpunished? When we act like everything is fine and no harm is done, we stage a theatre-like lifestyle, behaving artificially toward human kind. Albert Einstein (1879- 1955) stated, "Only a life lived in the service to others is worth living."

Could humans have this mean-spirited phase, believing in their power and influence so much that they would defy nature, life, and even God? Could individualism, and indoctrinating an ideology of such thoughts and beliefs have anything to do with the many things that malfunction, leaving society to bear the pain and suffering the dire effects that ensue? Why are we being muzzled and not allowed to address the real issues in our lives, to seek what is right and what is wrong, and to let justice prevail so that we just might have peace in this world?

If only we could realistically care enough to promote the discussion of the culture of individualism at a grassroots level, to examine its pro and cons, and the ramifications that we all have to face in our daily lives. Then it would be soon be apparent that its troubles are much more than its benefits, or any positive outcomes that it might offer. This school of thought systematically provides anyone with the attitude and the rivalry to bulldoze their way out and to conquer everything, all in the name of profit and self-interest. It simply shuns and divides people from each other, similar to solitary confinement. It leaves behind nothing but bitter consequences and hurts. Adam Smith said, "No society can surely be flourishing and happy, of which the far greater part of the members are poor and miserable. "The irony is that we are conditioned to believe people of this kind are blessed, and perhaps more favored by God. It should not be hard to realize the destructive power of such a mentality, in thinking one is so immune to the hazards and the troubles that would eventually reach everyone, both the rich and the poor. When speaking of climbing to the top of a financial culmination of power, it becomes clear that our common wealth is not so common anymore. Those at the bottom rungs of that power are devoured by the super-rich and their influence. Even the governments give in to their unjustified demands, because of their mighty positions, leaving the common man depleted of his God-given natural resources.

Adam Smith says, "Civil government, so far as it is instituted for the security of property, is in reality instituted for the defense of the rich against the poor, or of those who have some property against those who have none at all." We forget what has endured and sustained the capitalist system for probably three hundred years so far. It has been its outlook on fair and just competition, and a laissez-fair attitude. Its pioneers did remind people about the dangers of hoarding and concentration of so much wealth, and that power that would most definitely lead to financial tyranny, as it has now. When neither common man nor his environment are safe from the perils and wrong actions taken against them, perhaps we are all headed toward becoming an endangered species in the near future? Is it our pride, or our ignorance, or both, that does not allow us to see the obvious trouble facing us all? Modern society is acting just like an autoimmune disease, like a cancer that destroys the cell, its very life, and the foundation that supports and sustains it.

Joseph Campbell asked, "<u>Is the system going to flatten you out and deny you your humanity, or are you going to be able to make use of the system to the attainment of human purposes?</u>" If only we could stop disenfranchising our feelings, and truly understand we are not cold-blooded reptiles, and not to be dealt with as such. Then and only then, we will perhaps be able to collectively and constructively deal with other decisive issues and problems facing mankind. John Maxwell states, "Self-centered leaders manipulate when they motivate people for personal benefit. Mature leaders motivate people by moving them for mutual benefit." In addition, Josh McDowell notes, "We've had a major shift in what truth is and where it comes from. We've gone from being God-centered to self-centered, from being objective to being subjective and from being internal to external."

James A. Baldwin once said, "The most dangerous creation of any society is the man who has nothing to lose." Joseph Stieglitz, a Nobel Prize winner in economics adds, in an interview with Amy Goodman, "The only sustainable prosperity is a shared prosperity." I say that when we undermine a huge part of our productive forces who are responsible for a healthy economy and financial well-being, and hence, for our livelihood, it will come back to haunt us. We are practically getting rid of the middle class, destroying small businesses, and have forced the working class into idleness and hopelessness, where the ramifications are creating a hostile and violent society.

We are in urgent need of retrieving our strength and belief in divinity and in asking God for a piece of heaven upon our planet Earth, to include social tranquility everywhere. In this heaven, no one would live in fear and everyone would be able to have his or her deepest wishes and desires answered. Maintaining it would be for good cause—to bring about love, true friendship, happiness for all, and a financially savvy nation where financial disparity would not divide us. Fredrick August Von Hayek proclaims, "The principle that the end justifies the means is in individual ethics regarded as the denial of all morals. In collectivist ethics it becomes necessarily the supreme rule."

Unless we are able to sensibly answer the important question of "who I am as an individual and who are we really, as groups," it would be a waste of time to respond to other questions that might seem necessary to make a better life. Not having a clear answer would deaden any other attempt that might help remedy our human suffering. We need to awaken to the underlying unity and true cause beneath the reality of the world we observe. We are inextricably restrained in a world where we have split into subjects counterproductive to the objectivity of Mother Nature and cosmic consciousness. Because in today's lifestyle, self-realization often emanates from material belongings and our attachment to the physical world. This makes social work and collectivism look like utopia, where a belief in "all for one and one for all" seems like a farce and unrealistic. Hoarding wealth creates a shift in our social status, where we operate behind veils of greed and self-centeredness only to identify with those in our economic rank. Hence, the eyes of wisdom need to open up to the neuroplasticity of the brain; new grooves should form upon our brains where thoughts are reshaped and new ideas emerge, to make a profound state of consciousness possible. When our brains are rewired to transcend and acknowledge the bigger picture, this is not utopia, but a reality in accord with the cosmic energy of the Mother and in tune with the generosity of Mother Nature. We are undeniably part of this energy and can use it to authenticate our self-realization, fulfilling the true meaning of who we should really become.

Swami Yogananda, speaking of Jesus of Nazareth, said: "The saviors of the world do not come to foster inimical doctrinal divisions; their teachings should not be used toward that end. It is something of a misnomer even to refer to the New Testament as the "Christian" Bible, for it does not belong exclusively to any one sect. Truth is meant for the blessing and uplifting of the entire human race. As the Christ Consciousness is universal, so does Jesus Christ belong to all." He then continued to say that "In titling this work The Second Coming of Christ, I am not referring to a literal return of Jesus to earth....A thousand Christ sent to earth would not redeem its people unless they themselves become Christ like by purifying and expanding their individual consciousness to receive therein the second coming of the Christ Consciousness, as was manifested in Jesus....Contact with this Consciousness, experienced in the ever new joy of meditation, will be the real second coming of Christ—and it will take place right in the devotee's own consciousness."

As emphasized previously, life is like a jigsaw puzzle where we need to cooperatively put the pieces of the puzzle together to come up with the beautiful tapestry that is meant to provide enjoyment for everyone. It is not like a game of chess where our intentions are to destroy everyone so that the kings and the queens of our times, the corporate capitalists and the very source of our miseries, can survive. We should not lose touch with the reality of who we are, and we must stop exploiting the less fortunate and the poor in the name of power and influence.

We need to change the parameters of self-reckoning and prioritize the realization of what we can collectively accomplish when we become part of a human movement—one in which miracles can truly happen. Diligent efforts to know one's self and what we stand for in the name of humanity are important prior to registering in the mind of cosmic conscious; in this we shall be remembered by generations to come as the unforgettable marvels of our time. We must realize that we have a much more powerful and effective voice to raise questions and get the right answers when we are part of a movement. Why so many wars of aggression? Why so much military spending, since so-called evangelistic foreign policies have left behind more human grief, pain, and suffering for the very people you are trying to save? Why plummet so deep into supporting the lunatic dictators that murder, maim and torture their own citizens as we hug them, just because they are allies? What about forcing others to fight us head on— where is the morality, the solace and the human rights in that? Why do we allow profit to be valued above life, when thousands perish worldwide every day because of extreme poverty and hunger? Does no one care?

And at home, why are so many are unemployed without a job to sustain them? Why are we compromising on education and training in essential skills? Why are there no meaningful social safety nets to replace insecurity, fear and anxiety—because a society can become morally bankrupt when hunger and homelessness take over. Why are millions incarcerated, with no funds allocated for proper therapeutic and professional help so that so-called criminals can be remedied? Why not restore the true meaning of peace and justice, where human rights and liberty could actually mean something? Why not stop deep pockets and influential lobbyists from pouring money into campaigns which are meant to have adverse effects on people? These serve only the interests of the very few in reaching their vicious objectives. Why not create a more humane society where so many do not have to become inhumanly imprisoned? The system is so incredibly wasteful with impunity for the culprits causing it while the real criminals continue to steal big money. And why not stop global warming, in light of scientists' overwhelming requests and billions of people pleading for help? Why not implement systematic and decent universal health care for everyone to have access to when they become sick or really ill? If we are to preserve liberty and any democracy at all, then why not cooperatively insist on more funding for education, since learning at an early age is the very foundation to understanding democracy, peace, freedom, and our economic well-being?

Education, literacy, and civility of mind and manner must be invested in, since ignorance can be ruthless, like a cancerous agent eating through the very health of a body. Why are there so many corrupt interests at the corporate level? Without a doubt, this has left muddy footprints on the spine of our society. These legitimate questions need fair and decent answers, otherwise we will keep chasing our tails without realizing the essence of our very existence and why we are here. Many come to this world and leave not fathoming what happened— they are blind as bats, acting indifferent to their environment and mankind, not picking up on the power of pluralism. Oscar Wilde puts it this way, "We are all in the gutter, but some of us are looking at the stars." My thoughts are that we are nothing but animals with instincts when newly born, but are endowed with gargantuan potential for becoming human beings. Imagine if those miracles of potential are constructively put together to act in concert. I promise you that mountains can be moved, and we can reach where no man has ever dreamt to conquer.

We have the ingenious traits to gradually transition into human beings, with a God-like nature, just like silk worms that gradually turn into butterflies. It is assumed that we have adequate conditions for such changes to take place and good opportunities available to us. Envisage a beautiful tree bearing delicious mouthwatering fruit. Without sunshine, water, good fertilizer, and a decent gardener, the tree would wither away and die. Galileo Galilei stated, "I do not feel obliged to believe that the same God who has endowed us with sense, reason, and intellect has intended us to forgo their use." I believe that it is so very essential to give wisdom and reason a chance during these troubling times, where humanity and the entire planet Earth are in grave danger. Man is blinded with material hoarding, hypnotized with the accumulation of wealth and power, and is deemed to pursue this nonsense to the brink of hell.

Stephen Hawking notes: "life on Earth is at the ever-increasing risk of being wiped out by a disaster, such as sudden global nuclear war, a genetically engineered virus or other dangers we have not yet thought of." Yes, no doubt the potential of distinguished qualities lies in every one of us, but only develops if a viable and meaningful environment conducive to quality training accompanied by love and understanding, is available. And if one is bereft of positive education and deprived of a decent and friendly atmosphere in which to learn, with no proper role model, then it is difficult to cultivate goodness and expect reliable results. No one should be marginalized from having a good chance for advancement, where professional and caring instructors are present to administer to all without disenfranchising anyone.

Human behavior can undergo metamorphosis to reach its peak of higher self, if a decent enough atmosphere offering good opportunities is furnished. Such an environment is critical for success. We need to wake up and comprehend that we are dealing with a multifaceted, very complicated creature called a human being. It is a ruse to perceive or accept that some people are genetically programmed, that it is in their very DNA to be evil. That could not be any further from the truth. It's a hideous analogy and deliberately set in place to deceitfully assess the nature of mankind. We might, however, have the potential to morph into a demonic personality if abused, neglected, and treated like an animal.

This whole paradigm shift of nurturing must take place in order to prove that we have the phenomenal potential to grow and become separate from what which we are born into (animals with instincts). If we are not paid attention to, or are deprived of the right circumstances to dig out the omnificent powers within us, if we are not skillfully coached, then we simply kill the potential. It should become very questionable for one to carry the hallmark of a true human being if not properly nurtured within a constructive atmosphere. The most probable outcome would be a beastly character, if not worse. Now you are dealing with an animal that can think and purposely plan to do wrong, especially when not attuned with or in full grasp of moral standards where ethics and virtues prevail. This can exacerbate the whole situation, negatively affecting everyone within their reach. We have a great chance to attain solace and to alleviate most of our pain and suffering as human beings. If decency in character with proper etiquette and kindness cannot play a significant role in our society, we therefore deviate from the norm and perpetuate the worst.

We are emotional beings who can do an ocean of good if properly tapped into. If our higher self is encouraged, sought, and loved within a friendly environment, the best in us can be truly manifested. William Shakespeare said, "We know what we are, but not what we may be." Ralph Ellison said, "When I discover who I am I will be free." Socrates believed "that knowledge was the ultimate virtue, best used to help people improve their lives." "The only good is knowledge and the only evil is ignorance," he said. Socrates believed that people made immoral choices because they did not know any better, and did not have knowledge. Unless they examined their lives and gained wisdom, people would continue to make mistakes in ignorance. Socrates adamantly believed that instead of valuing money, power, influence, and worldly prestige, we must honor and value wisdom and knowledge more than anything else. Even when his life was on the line, he proclaimed, "while I have life and strength I shall never cease from the practice and teaching of philosophy, exhorting anyone whom I meet after my manner, and convincing him, saying: O my friend, why do you who are a citizen of the great and mighty and wise city of Athens, care so much about laying up the greatest amount of money and honor and reputation, and so little about wisdom and truth and the greatest improvement of the soul, which you never regard or heed at all? Are you not ashamed of this?"

The need for many to survive has prevailed by accepting that violence is as common as darkness, and grasping atrocious behaviors mistakenly considered to be part of the human genome. This is so sadly taken as the blueprint for who we actually are, and unfortunately believed to be part of human nature. The question is: should climate destruction, wicked poverty, ever more rape and murdering of innocent masses of people, genocide, wars of aggression, potential nuclear war, homelessness, provocative police brutality, financial insecurities, and exponentially rising displacement and refuges, be part of our human tenets and modernization, implemented in the 21 century? Just because we as individuals believe we are safe and secure, we are made to believe that what happens to the rest of humanity should not really matter. Yes I am sure there are a lots of "I prays," and "I hope so's," and tons of well-wished rhetoric, but you and I and the entire world know that is not going to help millions living in hell unless we collectively fight the demons of division improvised in the name of God and mankind. We need to solidify a global constitution and mandate protection from the flaws of blinded corporate capitalism and their hideous puppet lackeys of war and destruction.

This is the harshest reality for many open-minded societies to deal with, as the grueling side effects of crime weighs on conscious minds and vigilant souls to up rise against waves of corruption and abuse of power. This has beguiled nations into complacency and is molding them to believe that this is how human life started. Any inquisitive mind should be implored to ask whether these ugly themes and uncalled scenarios of violence are not purposely structured. Why, then, further fortify and design plots against humanity by spending billions of dollars to encourage them to build a culture of unrestrained ferocity and madness, facilitated through mainstream media and Hollywood-style propaganda?

Feeding the man of the twenty-first century within the culture of modernity should contradict anecdotes, fictional methodology, and manufactured stories of violence. These only alienate him from his potential to love and care for others, subtly validating his beastly nature. This does not identify with civilization. He must also realize that the fundamental cause that drives humanity to perpetuate irreparable harms is greed. Greed should be put on a short leash, rather than being rampantly urged. If not managed, this dynasty of action will annihilate what we know as life on planet Earth.

We are taught by society to masquerade civility and to delude ourselves and others by believing that prestige in technology and advanced science should be a good enough reason to claim a rich humane tradition within an ethical context. This, however, could not be any further from the truth. We should stop these shenanigans of hypocritical behavior and resist heading the wrong direction, naively perceived to be our correct destiny and contrary to belief in a life with purpose.

Essay 3
The Holy Role of Feminism in a
Corporate Capitalist Culture

We need to wake-up to the sacredness of feminism, and in retrospect look at this marvelous entity and her life-producing attributes. In ancient mythology, she was known as the goddess of birth and fertility, especially within agrarian societies. In Greek mythology, feminism was known by its Goddesses' qualities; the goddesses were revered not just as empty symbols, they were meant to uphold women's positions in the ranks. The following list illustrates many, but certainly not all, of these goddesses:

Iris – the goddess of rainbows
Metis – the goddess of wisdom
Nike – the goddess of victory
Lachesis – the goddess of fate
Hestia – the goddess of home and fertility
Harmonia – the goddess of harmony and concord
Hebe – the goddess of youth
Themis – the goddess of divine order, law, and custom
Tyche – the goddess of fortune and prosperity
Phea – the goddess of nature
Astraea – the goddess of justice
Aphrodite – the goddess of love and beauty
Erato – the goddess of love and poetry
Demeter – the goddess of harvest
Hemera – the goddess of daylight
Hera – the goddess of marriage and family, and wife to Zeus

Nemesis – the goddess of retribution and revenge

Urania – the goddess of astrology and astronomy

Hygea – the goddess of cleanliness and hygiene

Nyx – the goddess of night

Eos – the goddess of dawn

Elpis – the goddess of the spirit of hope

Gaia – the goddess of mother earth

Alectrona – the goddess of the sun

Ache Lois – the goddess of the moon

Eileithyia – the goddess of childbirth

Brizo – a prophet goddess and protector of mariners, sailors, and fishermen

Mania – the goddess of insanity and death

Melpomenme – the goddess of tragedy

I am certain these symbolic and godlike attributes and distinguished characteristics meant divinity on behalf of females, unless the Greeks were intoxicated and unquestionably ignorant. This must not have been the case, because they were one of the most prominent and civilized nations of their time, as were the Egyptians, who revered women equally if not in higher regard.

Feminism is innately endowed with love, softness, empathy, kindness, tolerance, compassion, beauty, peace, and with life-bearing productivity. A human mother identifies with Mother Earth through the bearing of life and sustainability, and by intuitively providing the parenting experience that a newborn is introduced to. Feminism and its interconnectivity with nature and life needs to be realized, since the image of the mother is undeniably linked to giving birth and nourishment, as by nature, motherhood is connected with nurturing and caring from the very inception of the infant's life. When we navigate through history, we can detect not only birth, nourishment, caring and compassion as being very much associated with the feminine, but also wisdom and intuition, as these qualities are an undeniable part of the female entity and motherhood.

In "*Goddesses: Mysteries of the Feminine Divine* (2013)," the book's editor, Safron Rossi, PhD, successfully organized documents from the Joseph Campbell Foundation, including Campbell's unpublished lectures, to highlight Campbell's dynamic understanding of the archetypal themes connected to feminine divinity. In particular, she noticed several main themes that Campbell linked with goddesses and the feminine divine:

1. Initiation into the cosmos and nature, especially through the elemental;
2. Constructs of time and space: goddesses have been a primary agent for revealing the ideas of immanence and eternity, and thus exist outside the bounds of ordinary, lived experience;
3. Transformation: most notably guiding the life cycle from birth to death; and
4. Energy consciousness: developing a deeply felt sense of the "aliveness" of all life.

We are suffering from a deficiency of wisdom. In our search for meaning, which is wrongly directed and misidentifies many important aspects of our life, the female role should be ever more present, because women contemplate vital issues with regard to what plays a significant roles in their family and work lives. Women are by nature patient. They go through nine months of pregnancy and they put up with many restless nights to keep up with the well-being of crying babies. They can multitask by nature, they have nurturing qualities, and are attentive to their entire family's wellness. Women are intricately delicate in their physical anatomy and their emotions, and completely dedicated to their children.

Many companies recognize female employees as high-ranking, especially in retail industries, where productivity and the need to maximize a firm's profit is at stake. Their natural attributes and abilities are very conducive to the efficiency of public relations and in possessing tranquility of mind and manner when referencing clients and customer satisfaction. They communicate with professional etiquette and with tolerance—definitely a plus when trying to avoid problems and in peacefully troubleshooting conflicting issues.

We need more high-ranking female prospects in charge of important vocations, because it seems with our progress in technology we have pushed wisdom aside, and its absence has created a civil vacuum in our life, tilting it toward too much violence. I am certain a more active role of females will mitigate this crisis to a realizable extent. One of the hallmarks of wisdom is to go beyond self-centeredness and pride; a wise person should search for meaning. It seems ladies are able to look at the larger picture when facing trouble, and are efficient in solving inadequacies such as in family budgeting, sometimes having only the bare minimum to work with. Females are much more awakened and sensitive to soul-searching, and meaningfully identify with others' pain and suffering.

Yes, wisdom is personified by female attributes, however we have to realize that even feminists bear difficulties in cultivating mindfulness when dealing with financial depravity or in being the victim of family violence. No one's interconnectivity can bear fruit when hungry and when loved ones' lives are seriously threatened. Despite many goddess-like qualities in human females, they are undeniably discriminated against even in this modern time of the twenty-first century. We ought to know equality is a virtue, an undeniable part of human nature. It is a necessity. It is as natural as electromagnetic force. Since we all belong to the same planet, misogyny must be condemned in every culture, no matter under what circumstance, either under democracy or tyranny.

Sociologist Sylvia Walby has composed six overlapping structures defining patriarchy; these structures take different forms in different cultures and different times:

> *The state:* women are unlikely to have formal power and representation
> *The household:* women are more likely to do the housework and raise the children.
> *Violence:* women are more prone to being abused
> *Paid work:* women are likely to be paid less
> *Sexuality:* women's sexuality is more likely to be treated negatively
> *Culture:* women are more misrepresented in media and popular culture

And I say, despite the fancy rhetoric by religion to uphold women's statuses in so-called "liberated and democratic nations," females are still treated as possessions. Subordination to the male species is promulgated and subtly indoctrinated (and hence echoed within) our culture and into the reality of women's lives. Patriarchy dictates that property and entitlements are inherited by the male lineage, whereas the female alternative, matriarchy, is suppressed. And I would like to further add that it is a great sin to portray women as sex objects, dehumanizing them into selling their bodies for the sake of daily sustenance, where so many sacrifice themselves for the sake of their loved ones' survival. As Brigham Young so cleverly stated, "You educate a man; you educate a man. You educate a woman; you educate a generation."

A thorough study of women through time from the past to the contemporary age shows a compounding exploitation of women, first being taken advantage of in a productive labor force, and then increasingly looked down upon in societies where male chauvinism and parochial superiority rules. This insatiability of cruelty to females must be stopped. Doors should be opened to women taking on higher employment and positions of auspicious power, in either the public or private sectors, to do the most good for society and the wellbeing of the masses.

It is noteworthy to realize that domination by men of women is found throughout most of human history, as far back as 3100 BCE. With the appearance of the <u>Hebrews</u>, there is also the exclusion of women from the God-humanity covenant, which has carried into other monastic religions such as Islam and Christianity. It is also of value to know that despite their horrendous and unreasonable animosities toward each other, and their ebullience, this trinity of monastic religions of Judaism, Christianity, and Islam stem from the same Abrahamic roots. The same father figure is the common denominator of each one, which makes one wonder why so there is so much discord.

In an interview with Bill Moyer, Joseph Campbell explained that the Hebrews killed all the goddesses in the history of mythology that referenced birth, fertility and nourishment, peace and loving, caring and kindness, leaving Gods of war like Zeus and Yawa as more of interest. With regard to religion, Joseph Campbell said, "<u>Every religion is true in one way or another. It is true when understood metaphorically. But when it gets stuck in its own metaphors, interpreting them as facts, then you are in trouble.</u>" The famous Greek philosopher Aristotle depicted females as morally, intellectually, and physically (even in terms of beauty), inferior to men, using male animals like lions, tigers, peacocks and so forth as examples of being more attractive. He saw women as the possessions of men; he believed that a woman's role in society was to reproduce and serve and obey men in the household, and emphasized the male domination of women as natural and virtuous.

Many sociologists have raised their pens in anger regarding the idea that patriarchy is natural, explaining that patriarchy evolved due to historical events rather than biology. In technologically simple societies, men's greater physical strength and women's common experience of pregnancy combined to sustain patriarchy. Gradually as technological advances, especially industrial machinery, took place, the importance of physical strength in everyday life diminished. In addition, the advent of contraception eventually allowed females control over their reproductive condition.

In her book, *Women Who Run with Wolves*, Dr. Clarissa Pin kola Estes draws further parallels between women and nature. Both share:

Keen sensing
Playful spirits
A heightened capacity for devotion
Relational tendencies
Inquiring spirits
Great endurance and strength
Territorial awareness
Inventive ideas
Loyalty

She writes, "Is it a coincidence that so many natural geographical features are personified as female? We feminize mountains, lakes, streams, rivers, trees and forests. Mother Nature herself is considered female, ruling with power and maternal care."

Patriarchy has traditionally influenced men to act masculine and "macho," showing little emotion, able to resist weakness, and encourages men to be leaders. Any man not meeting this standard risks finger-pointing and being labeled as having a "girly attitude," among other intimidating connotations. It is a great thing that at this stage of our lives, the beliefs of the majority are against sexism, racism, and other prejudicial criteria. This sets the landscape for freedom, democracy and human rights at a higher level, where the culprits are identified and are punishable by the law of the land.

And yes, there still exists many agendas against women which must be corrected, since many jobs are not accessible to mothers. On the average they are paid less than men, and on average, employed women's working hours almost double as compared to men's, since they have to take care of most household chores in addition to their responsibilities at work. The myth is that feminism has culturally prevailed where women's rights are equally preserved. This might be true to a certain degree because of the progressive women's movement, but is certainly not accurate in its entirety, as there are still compelling challenges for women to overcome in a culture that glamorizes and glorifies them into Hollywood-, or

Bollywood-style fame to maximize profit. So many women fall into such traps worldwide, idealizing actresses, singers, dancers, and wanting to be in the entertainment industry, but ending up in the wrong hands when human trafficking becomes their destiny. It is a widespread problem where the efforts of many humanitarian organization are sadly futile, since there are no fundamental, constructive, economic and cultural remedies. Even the legal system benefits from this evil trend of using women as commodities since they are literally exploited as a money-making machine. Finally, corporations propagate their products through sometimes distastefully ill advertising, abusing women's position by wrongfully portraying the role of females in many societies.

It should make any inquisitive mind wonder when eighty-five billionaires own more wealth than half of the people on planet Earth. Some hard-working women earn less than two dollars a day; this deprives them of the indigents that form the very basic necessities of life's subsistence. Thus I believe it is very difficult for women to think straight and bear wisdom, when they and their children suffer intensely from famine, malnutrition and many other horrifying situations imposed on them with impunity imparted to the actual perpetrators of such brutal crimes against humanity.

In *The Golden Notebook,* Doris Lessing points out:

> Ideally, what should be said to every child, repeatedly, throughout his or her school life is something like this: 'You are in the process of being indoctrinated. We have not yet evolved a system of education that is not a system of indoctrination. We are sorry, but it is the best we can do. What you arc bcing taught here is an amalgam of current prejudice and the choices of this particular culture. The slightest look at history will show how impermanent these must be. You are being taught by people who have been able to accommodate themselves to a regime of thought laid down by their predecessors. It is a self-perpetuating system. Those of you who are more robust and individual than others will be encouraged to leave and find ways of educating yourself — educating your own judgments.

Those that stay must remember, always, and all the time, that they are being molded and patterned to fit into the narrow and particular needs of this particular society.'

How well said by Ms. Lessing. It seems we are all relatively hypnotized and indoctrinated into a state of not questioning such blatant economic injustice where so few people can accumulate so much of the world's resources and wealth. This imbalance forces almost half of the world's population to live in deplorable conditions, given very little chance to improve their standing or the opportunity to explore their minds and talents for a better future. As a result, so many live and die in vain.

Our capitalist culture stokes the part of the brain that instigates impulse and instinctual behavior, not the part of our brain that relates to reason and wisdom. This is so the dire subjectivity of the wealthy can be accomplished without question, and their money is maximized no matter what cost. No moral or spiritual transformation can ever become materialized in such an environment, which not only encourages inequality and the exploitation of women, but many other cultural and social-economic problems facing humanity. Can the system and the corporate capitalists be the real causes of our human misery—the literal destruction to our civil and democratic life? They introduced the very issues of freedom, democracy, liberty, human rights and the pursuit of happiness into this country, saving humanity from the clutches of ignorance, religious backwardness, and despotic actions—where a renaissance into modern thought and belief was welcomed and embraced. Has capitalism run its course, serving now as not only an obstacle blocking human progress and prosperity, but also becoming a tyrant, obliterating anyone and anything in its path?

Basil of Caesarea, a 4th century saint, bishop and theologian who preached at length on the subject of wealth, coined the term "the dung of the devil," a phrase quoted by Pope Frances in reference to the unfettered pursuit of money. In my personal opinion, this term should more appropriately be applied to the multi-national corporations, as such corporations have effectively killed fair competition and abolished the free-enterprise system as we know it, annexing the whole globe by rampant use of the following tactics: neo-colonialism, exploitation, supporting wars of aggression, the killing and murdering innocent people, the rape and slaughter of women and children, illegal and deplorable exodus and forced migration, and the inhumane punishment of immigrants instead of extending welcome.

Trillions of weapons are sold each year to ignite or continue rivalries among puppet and dictatorial regimes safe-guarding their bosses' domineering positions in the appropriation of resources. More specifically, leaders kill for places that provide cheap raw materials, such as those loaded with a zillion gallons of oil and gas, or saturated with diversified rich minerals. Diamonds, gold, silver, copper and uranium and many other precious metals are usurped from defenseless inhabitants, ignoring the very fact that these natural resources are the only sovereign rights of its people. Such rights must be respected and not confiscated by exertion of force and treachery, as this practice deceptively violates the allegiance of faith and good business and does not recognize the real owners and citizens. They must be treated like any other legitimate suppliers and respected business men and women should—in an honorable and lawful transaction, which does not include theft.

Unrestricted capitalism destroys climate and causes widespread diseases through the production of chemically manufactured food, pollution of the air we breathe, and contamination of the water we drink. These resources are the very source of human existence. Poisoning them creates ethnic and national distrust, stirs the pot of ethnic cleansing, and manufactures socio-economic prejudices against women and minorities. Jobs are out-sourced, causing swift unemployment and resulting in the destruction of communities through recession, inflationary environment, and many other economic ills. Such ills create felons and violators, who fill prisons at the expense of tax payers' money.

Unemployment's ripple effects have practically forced poverty on people; many become separated and divorce due to resulting family violence. Huge disparities of income and intentional misallocation of resources leads to financial grief and class differentiation, forcing many to live a life of literal hell with no mercy. All of this and more, just because those in power "can." People should collectively demand the return of fair competition in the marketplace and push for global restoration of spiritual capitalism—a system that measures integrity and commitment as much as profitability. Another option is to push to implement other new ideas for a cooperative economic system, such as a system where freedom and democracy will be truly practiced at work; either this or acquire a progressive social democratic system, where neither socialism nor capitalism is the absolute; the key is balance.

More women need to be placed in positions of power. Women are by nature caregivers when not under the influence of male protégés; increasing this natural behavior in the economy will help to ensure that innocent lives do not have to perish so that a few capital moguls can live lives of extreme luxury. The prevalence of misconduct and betrayal from the top down has shaken the very pillars of social and economic trust in our society; a trust that must be relied upon to adhere masses of people together in upholding the law and a belief in the capitalist system and its institutions.

Because of calamities caused by inhumane foreign policies of many powerful countries, billions of women face horrific situations world-wide: single-family parenthood, widows who have lost their spouses in war-torn places, and sickness with no available medical doctors or treatment facilities. Hundreds of thousands orphans are left stranded and homeless, looking for recruiters of hatred to convince them that they belong. Of course these orphaned children are then indoctrinated and brainwashed into doing the unspeakable work of terror, or end up victims of human trafficking and dead or jailed. Millions of women are not employed. Many others are under-employed with inadequate pay, without education, or without marketable skills. Still others, living in war-devastated countries, are without shelter, medical care, and food or clothing subsidies of any kind. This war declared against God and humanity must be redirected toward the real propagators of sin and prejudice in order to halt the devastating effects on helpless commoners and innocent people. We must stop the permeation of these demonic foreign policies into foreign nations; most have done nothing wrong. We must stop hugging the real culprits, also known as our allies.

We must collectively mandate humanitarian resolutions, and call for urgent remedies to heal the very structure of the system through insightful Cultural Revolution. We are on the brink of total destruction: by potential atomic wars, terrorism, global warming, and perhaps bloody revolution, where millions are going to lose their precious lives if the conflict cannot be handled through peaceful means and common sense dialogue. In conclusion, I believe that if we had more women in positions of power, in both our public and private sectors, a much better fate would behold humanity. Violence and decimation of innocent lives would be far rarer, as females are tranquil by nature, and life-bearers, not life-takers.

Essay 4

Immigrants' Dance of Death

Lyndon B. Johnson said, "The land flourished because it was fed from so many sources—because it was nourished by so many cultures and traditions and people." Dennis Kucinich said, "I take issue with many people's description of people being "illegal" immigrants. There aren't any illegal human beings as far as I'm concerned."

It is bizarre when outrageous actions are performed against defenseless people in the name of upholding the law. These seemingly occult misconducts result in painful outcomes that are manifested against the most deprived and helpless masses of people, stripping them of their human rights and dignity, depicting them worse than the meanest villains and repeated felons. Not understanding this, most immigrants flee from despicable wars and hungers that crush the human soul; they run from the oppressive lethargy of not having any choice, or because of crippling economic criteria imposed up on them in the name of profiteering, ultimately delegating poverty to its inhabitants.

Neglecting unprotected people is not due to a momentary lapse of reason; it's about willful and conscious attempts to pass the bucket of irresponsibility where there is no accountability. Some are naïve that the root cause behind millions of people being displaced was colonialism, which embraced intervention and elimination, and the seizure of valuable properties and precious resources from their rightful owners. And since treaties were made without taking into account the inherent rights of indigenous and ethnic groups, they were forced to leave; settling colonialists simply took over. Their broken economic and governmental machines desperately in need of help, they first indoctrinated the world in the name of democracy and the rule of law, where in God we should trust is to preside—then looted, raped and exploited the natives and indigenous people by distancing them from their natural and human resources to the point of exhaustion.

The cynical choose not to see. It was because of industrial revolution and corporate domination, intertwined with colonialism and imperialism, that the world was transformed. Not through peaceful means, but by militarism, war and bloodshed, and absolute violence—which of course left vicious and horrifying side effects, including displacement of victims, behind for so many. Draconian practices are routinely taking place where fallacies are disguised by democratization, freedom, and human rights. For example, we invade other countries because of trumped-up charges against them, infecting the world with a war of aggression.

Since when are such sacred entitlements like freedom and liberty accompanied by bombing and murdering innocent people? Why is such brutal hypocrisy in action, when we could just as easily bring peace and positive change to victims of misfortune—upgrading their heinous living standards and allowing them to constructively participate in reconstructing their destiny? This is a win-win situation, destined for positive cultural change by bringing people closer to believing in one world and one government under God—where challenges can be surmounted, the world's environment free from hostility, and making our planet a safer place to live.

I am certain you know the answer, although the intent of those in power is evaluated only through monetary cost-benefit analysis. It so brutally leaves murder out of the equation, and the subsequent effect of homelessness by shamelessly counting the victims as collateral damages. It is so naive of you not to connect the dots when the almighty God punishes you with a painful death and horrifying sickness, or a bizarre accident beyond anyone's expectations.

Yes, I am talking about the so-called unlawful immigrants and refugees, who are the victims of horrifying and cruel policies implemented to punish them so that the exodus of helpless people is halted. This is undeniably the wrong way to resolve such an ever-present international problem. Many fervent nationalists, prejudiced citizens and extremists stand out like a sore thumb as they support ratification of the most backward and inhumane rules discriminating against these so-called illegal aliens, in essence, treating them like they are nefarious terrorists! Those arriving from other countries are irrationally evaluated and seen as problems, potential detriments to social order, even as future competitors for jobs. There is also a perception that they may also disturb citizens' tranquility and peace of mind. We forget that millions of so-called illegal immigrants are forced from their natural habitat and rural environments, which either have urbanized or are in the process of becoming metropolitan zed. These critics are entangled in the web of their own imaginations and by a culture of denial, not realizing the extent of damages that are caused by transnational corporations and venture monopolists. They do not see these as the actual causes of human misery and as the menace to the very fabric of our existence that they really are; in the meantime, huge companies pollute nature and destroy the life that sustains millions of species in the taxonomic hierarchy.

Corporations and monopolists have radically disturbed a vital balance, ignoring the importance of the life-bearing, nurturing, and dynamic alliance of man. They forget that humans are the last link in this intricate chain of command, and are ironically responsible for its preservation. We are in crisis mode, and surprisingly do not pay attention to the potential harm facing us. Unless we stop this "business as usual," including our addiction to war and violence and profiting at the cost of toxically contaminating the atmosphere—polluting the water and wiping out the soil from its vital nutrients—obviously nature's biodiversity and ecological systems will be eradicated. If we continue at this unprecedented rate, mass extinction of life-bearing plants and other catastrophic results are to be expected. This should awaken us all to lobby for the sequestration of carbon and other chemically deadly agents, providing natives a chance to restore and revitalize their means of subsistence through organic agricultural means, helping them with meaningful rehabilitation of the ecosystem, and in recapturing their natural way of living.

If not, perhaps we must then become consciously awakened by witnessing our own grief and anguish when we finally realize the loss of connectivity to our planet Earth; it's the only one we've got! We must reinvent what is to be human and actively take part in the sacred landscape of Mother Nature where we belong. Why do we act delusional by believing we have the self-efficacy to survive without our dependency on divine and resourceful nature?

We need to restore our intimacy with each other and Mother Nature, and stop this neurosis of individualism…showing off by means of high consumption and glamorous living. We should shake up corporate takeovers, which have directly caused indigenous people, ethnic natives, and refuges of war and hostile environments to flee from their homelands. Multinational corporations have eroded their very fabric life, having no regard for their well-being. As Carlos Fuentes eloquently stated, "Recognize yourself in he and she who are not like you and me."

Many wicked nuclear and atomic entities, as well as the fossil fuel industry, produce life threatening-products and then dump their killer waste shamelessly where they please—polluting people's water, sources of food supply, and the air they breathe. And because they are in cahoots with the corporate warlords, natives and indigenous are then left with no environmental laws to protect themselves. They become prone to a host of cancer-causing agents, ultimately stricken with deadly viruses and bacteria which generate previously unheard-of maladies. Because of rising sea levels, drought, and famine, their way of life and means of subsistence (traditionally gained through agriculture, fishing, hunting, and homeopathic medicine) is exterminated.

Many natives and ethnic groups unknowingly perform this "dance with death" as they depart to other desolate places, as they are left with no other options to live where they are. The other option is to migrate abroad to inhospitable and hostile places, where they become vulnerable to persecution and dealt with harshly, like they are wild beasts that deserve to die. They brave stormy seas and risk their lives trying to cross deserts and marshes, navigating forests and mountains, all the while migrating for survival and in search of happiness. If they are lucky enough to make it to the civilized world, they are paid the bare minimum for performing the lowest of occupations, which no citizen would touch with a ten-foot pole. The fear of getting caught while at work is ever present since they are stripped of any protective civil and labor laws, leaving employers to take them for granted, stomp on their rights, and leave them disenfranchised with no way to gain promising jobs or to unionize.

Some critics are impetuously cruel and ignorant. They are the arch enemy of reason. They cannot fathom debacles facing the international monetary system, which is shrouded in secrecy and is consequentially the real cause of poverty in many places. Natives are left with no choice but to take high risks by leaving their motherland. It seems these vehement perpetrators are infatuated with seeking heroism, expecting a sweet pat on the shoulder as they unleash vociferous wrongdoings against these little people—desperate human beings—with no remorse. These immigrants have already suffered enough; they come with hope of reparation and remedy, not the humiliation to which they are subjected.

Media and propaganda machines compound the issue by hyping up corporate scandal and, displaying their culture of denial, they mold favorite mental scenarios and societal approval against the forsaken immigrants of misfortune. These so called "illegal aliens" are seemingly postured as extraterrestrial and in need of retreating to their own planet, or else bear the consequences. It is a no-brainer to see that they are only lost human beings who have nowhere else to turn, who risk their very lives crossing rough terrain to take refuge in the civilized world and hope for a better future; that maybe one day with hard work, perseverance, and perhaps a bit of luck, they also can have a thin slice of the pie.

We must understand that human affairs encompass both choices and will, which makes human interactions (especially social justice, politics, cultural sensitivity, and other related anthropologic views) very complex matters. These matters can morph into dilemmas that demand rational thinking merged with syllogism and innate reasoning, known as "phronesis." Such methodology is distinguished from and often contrary to scientific knowledge, defined as that which one can perform in laboratory to assess a reliable findings, or "episteme." Ultimately, wisdom stands above all and is the pinnacle of savvy character. Insightfulness is leveraged through the combination of heurism (experience) with cognitive ability; everyone is gifted with this ability. Swami Prajnampad says, "To reach from opinion to perception, and from imagination to fact, from illusion to reality and from something that is not there to something that is, cultivates the way forward."

The trajectory of topics like immigration, racial inequality, national security, abortion, justice, assisted suicide, state execution, evolution, God and secularism, and marital and family violence are abstract and case sensitive matters, requires ingenuity, mental competency and clear conscience. These discussions must not be linked to preconceived judgments or opinions, as the subjects affected by these discussions might be burdened by the slightest chance of misrepresentation. I am not saying we all ought to be luminaries and scholarly minded characters; what I am hoping for is to stop feeding the beast of hatred and discrimination, as the inevitable victims are the deprived and the poor. I am encouraging open-minded thinking and ask that you not collude with those who are the real cause of these malicious conducts, as they abuse their power to do wrong, and are unbridled in self-grandiosities and narcissism. They have perhaps forgotten we live a life that stems only from our consciousness— that we are from one origin, one light, one life, one truth, one nurturing nature, one love and oneness, destined to return to where we came from. This means that life and death are bound to mysterious forces actively at work that are never to be known or figured out. Strangely enough, scientists and scholarly-minded physicists are pulling their collective hair out, trying to understand the one theory called "the theory of everything." Many saints and sages insist on the power of attraction and returning to the beloved source, which should beam human efforts toward unity in oneness, kindness, and compassion. All other theories that are outside of this realm will prove futile; the entire cosmos is predominantly subject to gravity and is able to sustain itself because of converging forces and gravitational strength, not by isolation and dispersion.

Having said that, the sovereignty to cast one's vote in complicated political, social, and judicial justice systems is meant to stem from training, education, and knowledge, as well as a firm grounding in high moral fiber, responsibility, and unwavering virtue. Biased results should not be tolerated where rightful decision-making is to be expected. No one's hopes should be shattered because of a wrong verdict, since justice should prevail in a fair state without any kind of prejudice or negligence. We should not allow anyone's accidental inheritance, birthplace, wealth, position, power and influence, or any other discriminatory merit, to play a role in skewing judgment toward the abuse of others. Such abuse can manifest in many ways: physical and metal manipulation, physical enslavement, the exploitation of those less fortunate, and the ultimate denial of civil and human rights. In God's name, all men are created equal and ought to be treated the same, not labeled as worthless commoners that can routinely be taken advantage of and belittled.

Immigrants must not be condemned to live an oppressive life. Billions of the poor are victims of Russian-roulette-type scenarios with respect to when, where, and to whom they are born. They become the victims of hate-mongering groups that embrace racial and nationality inequality, who label them with appalling language and in repulsive terminology. Such groups choose not to care about refuges of war and victims of unemployment and economic disasters, famine, heavy flooding, tsunamis, earthquakes, human trafficking and other horrific situations. They believe that no reliable solution is available, and as a result many people become horribly wasted in anonymity and silence. Internationally-known human organizations should realize this, and must prepare to provide meaningful safety nets to sustain tragic-stricken people as they fall, rather than holding them in detention centers to punish them even more.

Many xenophobes behave with indifference, manufacturing justifications for their beliefs, which allows their conscience to squeeze their targets into bearing irreparable damages and harsher repercussions, even death. Since often there is no accountability and because willful irresponsibility is taken so lightly, many human beings have to suffer.

Let's not be deluded and naïve in who is behind these riddles and quandaries that are purposely designed to plague humanity. They enthrall the common man through axioms in social and economic agenda; the common man does not comprehend the devil in the details— tricky doctrines filled with fine print, deliberate mind-bending mysteries, and paradoxes beyond imagination.

How can we attest to having reached the age of consciousness when we treat others as atrociously as our demented attitude allows? Should we not have a panoramic view into the fact that global and transnational corporations have mushroomed and are ever-present in the setting of this agenda? Why then should any enlightening mind not question why many natives and developing nations are controlled by the fear of fascism, where hierarchical and dictatorial rulers dominate and prevail over the rule of law? We ought to know that most dictators are literally puppets in alliance with idle hands, backed by internationally powerful and corrupt minds who make sure that helpless citizens have no right to control their destiny. Their actions should remind one of the horrors of colonialism, which is identical in ruthlessness, only presented in a different fashion. Similarly, people are manhandled and even imprisoned, pushed through phony referendums to vote on issues which have already been decided.

Just take a look around you; modern slavery can be witnessed every day by the following conglomerates: energy companies, oil and gas trusts and cartels, bank holding companies and "too big to fail" financial corporations, internationally-based gold, diamond and mining firms, infrastructure and real estate corporations, automobile industries, global electronic software and hardware corporations, industrial and textile companies, pharmaceutical companies, food industries, agricultural monopolies like Monsanto and the like, marine and seafood companies, and aviation and branches of hostile military industrial complexes situated in many regions of the world. Multinational corporations force their way into these resourceful places, supposedly because illegitimate debts, known as venture capital funds, have supposedly been defaulted on. Companies then swoop in with the luxury of not paying taxes, and usurp raw materials and cheap labor to accomplish their monetary goals. There is no penitence; in fact they have smiles on their faces as they raise their fingers to show the sign of victory, all the while exhibiting satirical solidarity and cooperation with the populace.

My complaints are not under the premise of investments made and resources being exhaustively annexed due to billions of funds being shifted electronically and transferred without people's consent. It is more about depriving natives from sharing in what is rightfully theirs, forcing them to austerity and ominous pauperism, leaving them with no choice but to migrate elsewhere. And objections are not fomented to protect natives and ethnic groups by backing constructive business practices and encouraging their active role in balance and moderate modernization. It is about the rule of law being under siege and ordinances at hand being improvised to benefit the ruthless invaders and the gold diggers, who intimidate, harass, nab, and even murder anyone who would dare to contest their manufactured consent and supposedly the rule of law. Dissidents are labeled as traitors, sellouts, and a multitude of other demeaning connotations.

One can be as complacent as one wants to be. In not getting proactively involved, one concedes to resolutely assisting such tragic actions as: genocide and ethnic cleansing, terrorism, increasing prevalence of crimes, religious controversies that ignite strident animosities, economic disparities, money laundering and the evil of insider trading, unemployment, sweat shops, poverty, drugs and human trafficking, racial inequality, wars of aggression, racial supremacy, child labor, child abuse and pedophilia, honor killings, gender bias, misogyny and prejudice against women, counterfeiting goods (not excluding medicine, surgical instruments and tools, automobiles, even aviation and airplane parts), global warming, immigration, police brutality (police acting an occupational force, serving those with prestige rather than justice for all), the abuse of law with no due process, legal anarchism, a racially-biased criminal justice system, wrongful death and incarcerations, GMOs and chemically-infested foods, bacteria and brain-eating amoeba infiltrating our tab water, water shortage, population growth, gang-related problems, extremely dangerous gas drilling known as fracking, character assassination, espionage, profiling, support of dictatorial and inhumane regimes, religious extremism, racist fanatics, organized crimes, organized cult groups, Nazism and other hateful networks.

Immigrants are introduced to a prosthetic way of life, augmented with hundreds of tumor-like agents eating on the human body. These shenanigans and madness of lifestyle should remind us of the hell promised if we do not behave. And we are not behaving, as evidenced by many who practice in the name of Beelzebub (the prince of darkness.) With all due respect to Jesus, our mighty prophet and savior in heaven, we are now immersed in an emergency situation that cannot rightfully wait on the second coming of the Messiah. We must rescue God's children from sufferings manufactured in the name of power and profit, resume our wisdom and reasoning to acknowledge and resolve these predicaments amicably, and uphold enlightenment and compassion instead of bombing and military interventions compounded with crippling and inhumane sanctions.

We need spiritual practicality and not as much holy book literalism, so people can actually find some relief when still breathing, and do not live and die in vain. Assistance in the name of God should not be deferred in this life, simply referring human beings to the next life and the promises of heaven and living happily ever after. Masses of people are literally destitute for help now and not later. We are in need of moral transformation where humanity can claim its true nature. The mechanization of life has separated us all from our oneness with Mother Nature, leading to materialism and consumerism, ultimately undermining the evolution of consciousness. We have forgotten (or perhaps we no longer care) that life is about cosmic consciousness and the sacred energy that is the experience of the human body.

We should diligently pursue practical solutions and protect what in God's eyes is right and dignified, abandoning deplorable thoughts and demonic apparatus now. Let's not be overwhelmed with our might, but awaken to the historical fact that empires have risen by insisting on expanding, conquering the world for one reason or another through slandering others, and looting and annihilating them—but they have fallen from their past glory. You might say "why should it be different now?" And I say that it must make a difference since our prefrontal cortices have evolved and matured enough to know better, and certainly to discern right from wrong. The propaganda and media machines bulldoze us into believing that we live in the age of civility, where peace, human rights, freedom and democracy, justice, liberty and the pursuit of happiness should be the essence of humanity. If that is true and they are not hypocritically posed, then these neo-colonist behaviors and the "dark ages" mentality of the hegemonies must stop.

By the way, the real meaning of the word "hegemony" as defined by dictionary is: "the preponderant influence or authority over others: domination, the social, cultural, ideological, or economic influence exerted by a dominant group." If that is the case, why would anyone in his right mind contest such high values as establishing a decent culture of thinking and influence, where scared principles like freedom, democracy, human rights, justice for all, liberty and the pursuit of happiness exist? Why not embrace competitive and fair economic practices, free enterprise with a robust and productive market, and above all, belief in God? We should be thrilled to be governed under such rules! Imagine a world where no military or police intrusion on people's sovereignty is allowed, and where the civilized rule of law is applied. No monopolies or manipulative financial interactions, and supply and demand can dynamically maneuver and exponentially grow. Hence, a hegemony that is impregnated with modern and humane ideas, and which is ready to deliver a better life, should be welcomed. This can happen if our mindsets and attitudes, our behaviors and our habitual beliefs, undergo dynamic and constructive changes. The cost-benefit analysis can no longer sacrifice human beings to greed and profit. New knowledge then becomes integrated as a dominant mutation as we embark on a new learning curve, the wisdom of which becomes innately learned and truly understood.

If this possibility exists, why should any mighty nation resort to bombing and destruction, and the killing and murdering innocent life? Why abuse its power by taking as its victims weak and forsaken souls who seek refuge under her wings? Social issues and the intricacy of human interaction rightfully calls for civility of mind and manner, which should be preserved for those claimants and the proponents of a progressive world. Some of them have brave hearts and take huge risks to venture toward the probability of achieving great tasks—tasks intended to save humanity from the clutches of ignorance, and sacred deeds to ensure that groundbreaking social criteria are positively manifested. They crave a life which is meant to be good, with the hope that everyone is truly recognized with decent human entitlement, so that they do not become just another statistic. Hegemony is not defined as bloodshed, or the intimidation of less powerful nations, or encroachment on people's rights by manifesting fear, controlling others, and usurping their natural and human resources. Policing through military invention, killings and mass murders in the name of democracy— that is certainly not the portrait of a Godly nation. There is strongly compelling evidence that man *wants* to live in peaceful coexistence, but in order for this to happen, he cannot be spurred or entrapped to do otherwise for inhumane reasons, or to increase monetary gain for the few.

Remember, remember always, that all of us, and you and I especially, are descended from immigrants and revolutionists."

—Franklin D. Roosevelt

Essay 5
Mind of God

In the apparent world, cause and effect play a convincingly practical role; should the denial of this relationship mean futility in the assessment of any scientific endeavor? Newton's laws of motion in the realm of causality are still the proprietor and pioneer of many experimental scientific accomplishments, but it seems they become irrelevant in the world of quantum mechanics as the world of the unseen epitomizes much different criteria. Even cutting-edge technology such as the most advanced magnifiers and complex telescopes have a difficult time making sense of intricacies in invisible life. It seems that the laws of physics, mathematics, and applied mechanics are unable to substantiate reliable answers from the infinite dancing subatomic particles. Scientists are rendered helpless to calculate homeostasis in particles smaller than the atom; the world of quantum physics has bewildered the magnificent minds of our time.

Let's start with the atom, which the Greeks believed was the smallest thing in the universe; they accepted that the atom was not divisible anymore. Modern science has since smashed that assumption to pieces, as in the past century physicists have discovered hundreds of particles more minute than an atom. These subatomic, indivisible units are called fundamental, or primal particles. For example, matter is composed of molecules that are made up of atoms that are made up of protons, neutrons, and electrons. While protons and neutrons can be further split into fundamental particles known as quarks and gluons, electrons are themselves fundamental—at least for now. As scientists and astrophysicists further sharpen their knowledge of the universe and deploy more powerful technologies, they will probably discover even tinier units underlying the universe. Fundamental particles of both matter and antimatter (in the form of antiparticles) exist. Corresponding to most kinds of particles, there is an associated antimatter antiparticle with the same mass and opposite charge (including electric charge). For example, the antiparticle of the electron is the positively charged positron, which is produced naturally in certain types of radioactive decay. Likewise, photons mediate electromagnetic force; gluons mediate strong force). Scientists currently believe that the tiniest particles are in the form of vibrating strings associated with the world of the unseen that sustains us. Just as our nervous system and senses are applicable to the visible world, then it is the infinite power of our brain and reasoning that should resonate with the unseen world.

For instance, oxygen cannot be seen and yet without it we can only survive a minute or two, perhaps less. The power of the mind, including our thoughts and memory, is what literally keeps us going—and yet this, too, is not seen. Can we ever see or feel our bones lengthen as they grow to make us taller? On average, sixteen to eighteen million magnificent thunderstorms occur each year, releasing adequate amounts of hydrogen and nitrogen to fertilize crops; this phenomenon is not seen by the naked eye, but it exists nonetheless. The vital energy activated in every animated being is not seen, and yet without it no life is possible; there are millions if not billons of other undetected agendas that can practically make us or break us. They are not visualized or detected by the naked eye, but they exist.

Our faith is not seen, but it is an inseparable part of our daily lives and a decisive factor in all that we undertake. For instance, we put our trust in the pilot's hand that air-lifts the jumbo jet we are in, or the taxi driver who transports us home. We take a leap of faith when we expect our parachute to open in mid-air as we jump out of a plane and then guide us to where we should land. A pregnant mother in good faith expects no complications during delivery and impatiently expects to hold her healthy baby right after it is born. And when soldiers are placed on the front line of nasty wars and in devastating combat situations, they expect to return to their loved ones. We expect to wake-up every morning as we lay in bed and sleep at night. Millions of other faith-based beliefs and the over-arching concept of "in God we trust" are the impetuses and the moving forces we cannot deny or do without; such forces are not seen, and yet are the essence and irrefutable attributes of our lives.

Mr. Michio Kaku, professor of theoretical physics and the co-founder of string field theory, states:

> The latest version of string theory is called "M theory" (M for membrane), so we now realize that strings can coexist with membranes. So the subatomic particles we see in nature, the quarks, the electrons, are nothing but musical notes on a tiny vibrating string. What is physics: physics is nothing but the laws of harmony that you can write on vibrating strings. What is chemistry? Chemistry is nothing but the melodies that you can play on interacting vibrating strings. What is the universe? The universe is a symphony of vibrating strings. And then what is the mind of God that Albert Einstein eloquently wrote about in the last thirty years of his life? We now for the first time in the history have a candidate for the mind of God. It is cosmic music resonating in eleven-dimensional hyperspace.

So first of all, we are nothing but cosmic music played out on vibrating strings, a membrane obeying the laws of physics, which are nothing but the laws of harmony on vibrating strings. But why eleven dimensions? It turns out that if you write theory in fifteen, seventeen, or eighteen dimensions, the theory is not stable. It caves in and has anomalies; it has singularity. It turns out that mathematics itself prefers the universe to be in eleven dimensions. Now some people have toyed with twelve-dimensional theory. A physicist at Harvard University has shown that twelve dimensions actually looks very similar to eleven dimensions, except it has two times, double times, rather than one singular time parameter.

What would it be like to live in a universe with double time? If you walked into a room you would see people frozen in a different time than yours, since you beat with a different clock, yet the clocks are running perpendicular to each other. That is called the F theory, "F" standing for the Father of all theories. It seems M theory in eleven dimension is the Mother of all string theories, since it works perfectly well in other dimensions.

Beyond eleven we have problems with stability; the theories are not stable, and they have deviations from the norm. They have singularity that kills an ordinary theory, so the laws of mathematics themselves force you into an eleven-dimensional theory. Also because this is the theory of everything, there is more room in higher dimensions to put all the forces of gravity, electromagnetics, and nuclear forces together, where the four dimensional space is not big enough to accommodate them all. When you expand into eleven dimensions, bingo, everything works well.

Currently cosmologists claim that the fabric of space and time based on Einstein's relativity theory has culminated in "gravitational wave theory," which might be the answer to how space and time originated. The collision of two black holes approximately 1.3 billion years ago—a colossally powerful incident detected the first time recently by scientists—resulted in gravitational waves that created a ripple across space and time. This was initially hypothesized by Albert Einstein a century ago when he plugged the idea of space and time curvature into studiously minded scientists in related fields. Hence, we should expect the impossible, since planet Earth is only a tiny cell in the body of the cosmos, leaving an infinite number of other planetary cells and universes still to be explored.

Despite physicists' grand attempts to search the unseen world for answers, they only become more puzzling and elusive, making a belief in the world of magic more credible. It is the world of the imperceptible that has actually made what is manifested in its entirety possible. It should remind us of the Big Bang Theory, which now is a dominant scientific fact. Prominent physicists claim there were no activities before the Big Bang—meaning no matter, no motion, no time or space, just the void (matter, motion, time, and space go hand in hand and operate in concert.) This should again affirm the view that life was produced from nothing, which is magical, isn't it? But then what we are incompetent to figure out is—what should be counted as magic or a miracle? This is obviously beyond our comprehension as humans, as our senses and nervous systems cannot comprehend "miracles" or deal with them in the name of science. But reason still questions: did the Big Bang just present itself out of the blue, from nowhere? Then that is magic, since no matter, no motion, no time or space could have ever existed before the Big Bang. To accept this is to believe that cause and effect as we know it in our physical world was not in existence then. Regression analysis can go forever unless a prime mover for all moves is manifested indisputably; in this one accepts an eternal God and therefore no longer needs a more detailed scientific explanation. If we do not accept an eternal God, then we need to accept a theory involving gradual movement and steady accumulation of matter, and an unsurpassed degree of heat so focused that potentiated singularity becomes a turning point, causing the Big Bang. This, by the way, would have led to a chaotic and raucous world. That is what any explosion must do, rather than implementing an utter miracle like a fabulously designed, majestically disciplined and displayed cosmos.

I am not hesitant to say that the incremental build-up of matter and the sharp concentration of explosive material and gasses is more favorable and attuned with scientific communities than a colossal eruption taking place out of nowhere. But then again if a gradual accumulation of matter was the case, then matter, or motion engulfed with time and space, must have existed before the Big Bang and ultimately introduced it. Either way we are sometimes left with no choice but to believe in nothingness. We would not be remiss in saying that it is the womb of nothingness, the so-called void, which is impregnated with all there is; everything is invented and relinquished progressively through the mind of man.

Knowledge and the technology of thought must mature enough to catch up to modernity, so that the power of reasoning and wisdom can adjust to the reality of our lives in different time parameters. Science has begun to ratify previously circumstantial evidence, setting the next stage for a further leap toward its predestined goal. We should sometimes accept the world of magic, where common sense does not make sense. Unless we believe the source of all things in good faith, no other option is truly available to rectify the inquisitive mind of man. The mind of God should be sought, since it is the only tantalizing path that can lead humanity to where it is destined. Significant cerebral maneuverability is to be very much expected, since ninety percent of the human brain's capabilities and cellular activities are still unaccounted for. This is comparably better than any other organism on planet Earth other than the dolphin; scientists believe that dolphins utilize twenty percent of their brain function by utilizing complex sonar, detecting through the use of waves and a sophisticated echolocation system.

It seems that in the gray matter of human beings' brains, billions and billions of potentially firing neurons can connect with other neurons through trillions of synapses to exchange information. This functionality has the capacity to spark superb and dynamic thinking ability in each of us: a gigantic network of information which perhaps in the near future can lead to extraordinary innovation for mankind to behold. Scientists acknowledge that to control one's environment and other people within it, one needs to have forty percent of one's brain cells working. God only knows what would happen if we were in control of one hundred percent of our brains, and geared them toward benevolence. Maybe then we would explode into the world of creating artificial intelligence where man seriously challenges his own robotic products, and delves so far into space and intergalactic events that science fiction and utopian dreams become the fundamental reality of high-technological breakthroughs.

In the same vein, religious parity can be tackled with distinguished intelligence, reflecting further truth. If enough information is made available, perhaps the stereotypical alien can then be depicted not as hostile, but as a positive force to help us wipe out the plagues facing mankind. The God of love and mercy must truly be manifested to save humanity from the brink of destruction. It is believed that if we are in control of twenty percent of our brain, we can feel the rotation of the earth, feel gravity, and feel the deepest memory in our brain. We can even hear the sound of bones growing, feel the taste of one's mother's milk, feel our brain and the heat leaving our body, and actually sense the blood moving in our veins. If we use our brain in this capacity we can control the beatings of our heart and remember thousands of our mother's kisses on our face. It is said that you can feel and remember the stroking of your cat or petting your dog from twenty to thirty years ago. In retrospect, you can remember your ancestors through genealogy and make sense of your lineage back to centuries ago, as though these individuals are actually in your presence.

The question is, why are we not able to expeditiously evolve to where progressive cerebral formation can help us enjoy the miracle of our brain's might? Let's say one is going through a surgery without local or any other kind of anesthetics; in this case all that one can feel is pain, which hinders every other passage in one's mind. Comparably speaking it is our hectic and painful lifestyles which have blocked our minds from playing a positive role and being the decisive catalyst to advancing vital agendas that should actually matter in our lives. We need an environment conducive to unlocking parts of the brain, providing access to untapped cerebral capacity previously unexplored. With increased capacity to learn, our brain cells can be produced at a phenomenal rate; development of knowledge and information to pass to the next generations can lead to these generations exploring the usage of one-hundred percent of the human brain. With the full use of the brain, our children's children could maneuver within parallel universes and access other planets, the stars, galaxies and an infinite number of universes.

We have created scales to make sense of the unscaled. If creatively pursued, this path should take humanity both into the future and into the past. It is not an overstatement to say that human beings will be empowered to experience not only the era of the dinosaurs but also the most advanced space age when this ability is possible, which will further support the activation of one hundred percent of the brain. Scientists predict, then, that humans will have the ability to disappear and reappear anyplace they choose, that we can be everywhere at the same time. As this possibility draws near, I am sure the rules of our daily engagement and how we interact also will dynamically shift and be re-evaluated.

It is said life was given to us one billion years ago; in retrospect we should have exponentially activated our brains to foresee the future, harnessing eye-opening knowledge to accelerate toward and progressively reach our destination. We should have known that ignorance would bring destruction and chaos, regressively affecting us all, throwing humanity off course so we are unable to fulfill our heavenly purpose. Meanwhile for groundbreaking future events, it is of grave importance to empower females as equally as males, if not more so. Society should recognize women's bright ideas and reference their energetic participation. We need to be much more receptive to feminism since by nature women are privileged with love and spirituality. Women can act as a huge catalyst, leading humanity to grasp oneness and reach collectivism, where the message of peace can be spread much faster. Femininity is the soft and efficient part of human nature. Because the overwhelming patriarchal culture has deviated so far from what is right, anchored in division and distrust, it has since brought our lives to the brink of destruction. We also need to stop the wild horse of greed that has an insatiable appetite for constantly demanding separation. Humanity should thrive for justified equity and a peaceful coexistence.

Knowing when the habitat is sufficiently nurturing and favorable, the cell will choose immortality through self-efficiency and efficient management. Leveraged with further evolution of the brain and a dynamic ability to expand human intelligence, we can not only control our environment, but the brilliance of our technology. Such technology should be competent enough to disintegrate the bodily cells at will when in transit, and to reassemble them as fast as the speed of light, with no change being physically felt. In other words, we can be "faxed," meaning our physical body disintegrates and then re-forms within a split second; soon this will not be science fiction anymore, but the reality of human beings' lives. It is no secret that fertile ground is absolutely necessary to cultivate our brains, this is with no doubt the essence of our success and the only vehicle to reach human destiny and the Promised Land. The seeds of desire and man's will are already planted, and shall guide us along our treacherous but joyful journey, where the search for meaning can be born into reality. Universal truths will manifest as we adjust to a new paradigm shift, becoming incrementally closer to our maker; under this paradigm, no man is an existential threat or ignorant enough to inflict pain and suffering on others.

Maybe then we will not be in the business of normalizing violence and encouraging crimes for monetary reasons. We will become free from stupidity and malfeasance, since ignorance is obliterated and replaced by the potent forces of enlightenment, compassion and wisdom. It shall be an era in which the power of collective consciousness allows us to truly see and marvel at the wonders of the universe and sincerely value what God has bestowed us with. Perhaps one day we will realize that the power of money hardens us and distances us from our creator, thus preventing us from truly perceiving the awesome power of the source of all existence.

We should in all honesty question how we can grow if we live in a procedural democracy and have the cosmetics of what democracy calls for, but actually carry out our actions with the brutality of a totalitarian government which also denies God. How can we truly unify and believe in oneness if so many are indoctrinated into various faiths that insist that no salvation is ever possible outside of their house of God, linked to their religion's dogma? Or when predatory lending, economic tyranny, and a few multinational corporations enslave billions, despicably playing God and condemning so many to live a life of misery and pain? Perhaps with the opening of more brain cells and firing neurons, we can discern enough to know there is only one path to God; a variety of lamps are lit by the same source of energy, the same electricity and the same light.

Everything and everyone is God's property; we should not abuse them, because when we do we are clearly messing with God's sovereign state. A divine energy flows through all of us with no exception or prejudice, just like the rain and a breath of fresh air, like the sun that sheds light on all, and the undeniable beauty of the moon and the stars. This energy embodies the breathtaking loveliness and vivaciousness of spring with its blooming plants and flowers, and other beneficent seasons welcoming us to new life forming in the womb of Mother Nature. Ever present in nature's majestic mountains, soothingly magnificent oceans and calming rivers, the energizing power of our creator is unmistakably present and witnessed. The beauty is not seen in the eyes of the beholder but in everything that exists; this is where the spirit of God rules. It is about time to understand that we can only identify these energies when presented in infinite forms, of which the human brain and our entire being is an inseparable part.

Every time that we excitedly trumpet a new scientific discovery, yet more cosmic energy is tapped into, getting us closer to the magnificent mind of our creator. Science provides the very means to seek an understanding of mind over matter; this understanding ironically reveals consciousness and the eternal mind of God in each and every step taken, since awakened energy in the visible and unseen world and the infinite cosmos sings a much different song. This knowledge should not be narrow-mindedly sought by fictionalizing it through Darwinism or any other obsolete scientific undertaking that presents a façade of so-called scientific findings. We need to foster our brains and advance our minds; this is the sole vehicle available to better serve the purpose of mankind. It is essential to relentlessly dig into our brains and harness the power of the collective mind, to work in concert to challenge nature since what we see is only the tip of the iceberg of what God has in safekeeping for humanity.

We need to value and respect Earth's precious resources and make certain to act as an extension of nature, not against it. Our Earth generously gives without exception. Because we are losing our connection with Mother Nature and the viability of our ecosystem, we are eradicating bio systems, and the animals, plants, birds and bees are in danger of becoming extinct. This is now abstract within our comprehension, yet it is eventually going to haunt us. We are behaving in accordance to our neuroses and acting with no conscience toward life-supporting organisms, the very foundation that keeps us as humans from becoming the endangered species ourselves. Many economists insanely and irresponsibly consider the following to be external costs in their models of external growth: rising sea level, melting glaciers, loss of rainforest, rising CO_2, pollution, excessive toxicity in the air we breathe and the water we drink, drought, famine and wild fire, destruction of marine life, tsunamis, floods, earthquakes, global warming and other phenomena. Considering them this way is clearly insulting to both God and humanity in the name of accumulation of wealth.

We desperately need a savior. Many prophets, mystics, saints and teachers have led the path to mystical experience, raising the level of human consciousness. Wisdom has played a huge role in awakening energy and intellectual capacity to overcome the darkness and difficult challenges of our times. We should also be grateful for every given moment and live our lives fully, becoming a beacon of hope and taking responsibility for saving others from the grasp of ignorance and misdeeds. We must avoid the cultural and economic differences that can keep us apart, and instead devote our caring and kindness to help hold us together. No bigotry of any kind should prevail, because we are all uniformly interconnected—from the working farmers that provide our food to the sanitation engineers who collect our trash, from the doctors who help us recover from illness to the scientists that sweat to find cures for rampant and epidemic disease. The peacekeeping missionaries and journalists who risk their lives in the midst of devastating wars share a connection with the soldiers who sacrifice their lives to keep peace and to maintain freedom and democracy. The teachers who teach us, the fire-fighters who save us, the nurses and caretakers, the scholarly minded scientists who lead the way, and so many others who devote their lives to fight a global evil of terrorism and war of aggression; we are all interconnected.

The prevailing culture of misdeeds has horrified human beings and will bring us all to the brink of extinction if not seriously dealt with through education, the power of reasoning and a sensible attitude, where God, compassion, acts of kindness, responsibility and receptiveness, empathy and understanding are all diligently pursued. I believe that education, literacy training and coaching, wisdom and the power of reasoning, and attaining information and knowledge are certainly the keys to human success and progress. Humanity is gifted with a cerebral capacity that is bound to expand as more brain cells are created, enabling billions of neurons to connect with trillions of synapses where they spark and fire to dynamically communicate. This expansion is sure to lead to more viable thinking and revolutionary ideas as the paradigm shifts into a new world with the potential for boundless advancement.

Scientists tell us that life started billions of years ago, where about four to five hundred million years earlier the first nerve cells came into existence with no sign of intelligence, just reflex in one neuron. Then, with more neurons, motion and movement started providing opportunities for more good things to happen. We cannot ignore the actual environmental cause and effect of a life-bearing atmosphere which manifested itself from the very beginning, making life's amazing journey possible. Experts in biology and related sciences say many species (with the exception of the dolphin, mentioned earlier) can only use three to four percent of their brains. Humans can on average utilize ten percent of their cerebral potential. Hence a system that values people's lives and well-being over the hoarding of money is needed to lay fertile ground, in order to best cultivate the intelligence and wisdom to save humanity from the clutches of ignorance. It is horrifyingly scary when people's minds are defensively occupied, resulting in such expressions as "life is not fair;" perhaps it is the mind of God that plays at such irresponsible acts of misfortune, including the game of financial Russian roulette with human beings. Absurd isn't it, since even a novice in economics should know that individual insatiable appetites for wealth should not be overlooked. As we leave all the tools and opportunities that play a very decisive role in people's welfare and wellbeing to chance, a game of probabilities is played with the global economy, resulting in a misallocation of resources and an absence of honest management. This has created a huge gap between the haves and the have-nots, which has exerted misery on so many people. The superbly rich and powerfully influential keep a stranglehold on the wealth of the entire nation, making "do or die" the reality for survival, as violence and a cutthroat environment becomes the norm in the so-called civilized world. The seeking of balance in monetary perspectives is mocked, and the hoarding of falsified money is naively applauded and glorified by tycoons of the world and cheerleaders of fiscal injustice. This attitude indicates callousness of brain and immaturity of mind.

A tiny, gradual increase in the number of opening brain cells will result in billions of neurons sparking trillions of synapses. This juncture inspires an apex of beneficial creativity in both the mental and physical make-up of humanity. The incremental escalation in firing brain neurons eventually takes a positive leap toward exalted endeavors, which should mean utter freedom from the life of idiocy where the mind of God is truly signified and curiously discerned. We need to awaken to the undeniable fact that unless we prioritize education and devote more resources to learning, we will be devoid of vital information which would expeditiously shed light on decisive issues of our time. Miracle-like events and breakthroughs beyond imagination can become reality, setting the stage for the next paradigm shift in human glory where glittering stars dance to celebrate the mind of man. In turn, mindfulness emanates wisdom, and the power of reasoning repels stupidity. It is not a far reach that substantive collective attributes lead to good deeds and virtuosity, making progressive tasks possible. Positive evolutionary perspectives will then convey civil communication and constructive dialogues.

We have within us a vast reservoir that can be tapped into by our subconscious mind, which restores thought patterns and behaviors to build modern and revered character, where barbaric and inhumane deeds are unanimously renounced. This allows an awakening of mankind and a preservation of the sanctity of higher self. If encouraged to survive, such enlightened character will strive to reach its pinnacle of success, meaning emergency accommodations for the acquisition of education, proper employment, decent housing, efficient medical programs, and free transportation. Genuine safety nets with no-nonsense financial plans will be put in place for retirees and seniors.

Ethology (a branch of scientific knowledge dealing with human character and its formation and evolution) can patent time parameters in accord with the era of prevailing human consciousness to promote civility of mind and manner. Making emergency accommodations is not a prerogative or optional, but is instead mandated wisdom—saving people's lives, well-being and prosperity, replacing violence with peace, justice, democracy, and human rights. In this realm, stoic actions are not encouraged, and sensitivity and compassion towards others' pain and suffering is positively reckoned with.

We must feel responsible to relentlessly seek practical resolutions to ill action and the actual causes of profound hurt, which have forced many to lose hope and integrity in the face of degradation and misfortune. Defective products are constantly disseminated, creating a restless, anxiety-filled atmosphere, and an uncertain institutionalized strategy that celebrates the segregation and disunity of humankind with expensive champagne and caviar. They choose to manufacture hatred to ensure the status quo and the enslavement of the wretchedly poor and destitute; cerebral deficiencies and economic benevolence in some have solidified the concept of divide and rule, rendering masses of people incompetent to perceive the truth. As a result, we as a collective are unable to expose the rampant corporate culture of falsehood and charlatanism, where God is toyed with to yoke dissidents in his name. In this, the poor are reincarnated to live miserable lives and condemned to be punished because of their character flaws and misdeeds in previous lives. The bottom line is that we need not undermine the mind of an omnipotent, omnipresent and omniscient God. The creator of Heaven and Earth is watching. God's final judgment will be crystal clear, imposed upon us with no ambiguity or prejudice, executed in a higher celestial court and conveyed through a precise and justified verdict.

Essay 6

Sociopath by Nature

Multi-national corporations have turned a substantive democracy into a cosmetically procedural one, indoctrinating people into believing that what they practice is authentic democratic ideology and as natural as can be. Clearly its economic and political domination are the best alternative since it has turned classes into a caste society. We choose not to see that their corporate monopoly has made fair and just competition an incompetent rarity. Through this means, distorted competition, class war, and alienation (from self, from society, from work, from nature, from appropriate and sensible production processes, from user-friendly public goods and services, and from God) is woven into the system. Citizens are malleable and forced into obedience by behavioral apathy acknowledged as rational, and cutting each other down has become the norm rather than building society in the name of humanity and cooperation.

Regrettably civil servant occupations are no longer admirable, and societies are encouraged to desire jobs that pay maximum salary regardless of whether those jobs are ethical or lead to a happy life. We are molded to be homogenized into a culture of ignorance. We are the credit card generation; consumerism and fashionable consumption defines what we know as the cradle of democracy. Critical and compelling issues are ignored as the dominant media and powerful political leaders have bewitched people into relapsing with no hope for a healthy recovery. Stephen King said, "The trust of the innocent is the liar's most useful tool." So, question more! Question conventional wisdom. Question the awareness (or lack thereof) of responsible authorities on significant issues such as the potential for nuclear war, climate change, and wars of aggression, deemed by Noam Chomsky and others as very troubling to mankind.

Senator Robert Kennedy, in his South African address on June 6, 1966, put it this way: "Each time a man stands up for an ideal, or acts to improve the lot of others, or strikes out against injustice, he sends forth a tiny ripple of hope, and crossing each other from a million different centers of energy and daring those ripples build a current which can sweep down the mightiest walls of oppression and resistance." In cultures where a monetary lifestyle is strongly valued, the agony is mostly felt by the indigents. The poor become victims in almost every walk of life, particularly financial, but due to the financial hardship, also in legal matters and within the judicial system. Lawyers are not there to seek fair play; many innocent victims end up sentenced to death by electric chair, or to lifetime imprisonment without being properly and adeptly represented. Doctors are another example. Many are not there to save lives, but to prioritize profit. Many ill people end up losing their lives because they cannot afford a cure. Then sworn financial officers who often hold all of one's financial stakes pull Ponzi schemes—swindling those who have placed their trust in them by taking uncalculated risks. The result? Homelessness without retribution. Perhaps with a slap on the violator's wrist.

We should realize that we have a real problem! We are not employed because of what we are, but are hired by those we know. We go to war not to establish peace, freedom, democracy, justice, liberty, equality or human rights, but for oil, gas, and precious minerals. We exploit gold mines and other valuable resources and commodities. We have a serious problem. When humanity is extracted from human beings and they are turned into objects that give a green light to the savage predators to brutally oppress, kill, maim, imprison and torture them in no man's land, we should realize we have a serious problem. When national resources are annexed by the powerful elites and the majority of people are denied a share of the pie, remaining at the mercy of multinational corporations and mighty elites for minimal subsistence, we need to recognize that we have a problem.

Economic dependency means no freedom for the poor. Since no reparations are ever rendered to the needy every time the monumentally rich decide to play fatal games with the powerless poor; since money is the driving force behind everything and can buy integrity, consciousness and justice; since currency forces its way into amorphous humanity and extracts the essence of virtue in man's character, we should know we have a problem. We should know that money has taken over—not as a medium of exchange, but as measure of wealth, prestige, power and influence. It has replaced deity, the sacredness of trade, kinship, interconnectedness and reciprocity, transforming the whole world into a machine. In a world where artificial desires are expressed externally, money has played a huge role in satisfying human wants. A madness in spending has become very addictive; many even kill for it, to quench their appetite. And on a global scale the powerful empire goes to war against the weaker nations to exploit and annex their wealth and valuable resources for the sake of money. This is conducted under so many false premises, mainly in the name of liberty, freedom and human rights.

When wars of aggression slaughter innocent bystanders and cluster bombs rain on innocent people, scattering their bodies all over as seen in the news, and you hear children, teens, and even adults screaming "cool"— we need to understand that we have a serious problem. Such wars are waged under the rationale of "exporting democracy"—as if implementing democracy needs no prelude or fertile ground to absorb such an intricately complex subject like democracy. When many have no roofs over their heads and have to search for food in garbage cans to survive, and no tears are shed in sympathy to find a solution, we should realize we have a serious problem. Our physical and theoretical eyes are blind to the urgency necessary to save ourselves from intrinsic harm. We are not catching on to the true hazards of the socioeconomic, cultural and psychological booby traps played upon society; these must be constructively dealt with and resolved. We should know we have serious trouble facing humanity.

Because these and many other conditions are definite signs of sociopathic systems, we are by nature required to awaken the many who are caught up in absent-mindedness before is too late for mankind. The system capitalizes on people's emotions, which I believe to be the strongest force within human nature. It is also often the most naïve, provoked by instrumental and very complex mental maneuvers that incite jealousy, greed, envy, vice, double standards, dishonesty, fear, anxiety, hate, moral indignation, and many other sickening feelings to accomplish its demonic strategy—all in the name of virtue. In *Man for Himself: An Inquiry into the Psychology of Ethics,* Erich Fromm puts it this way: "There is perhaps no phenomenon which contains so much destructive feeling as 'moral indignation,' which permits envy or hate to be acted out under the guise of virtue." It seems like an endless variety of malicious covert operations perpetrated globally by the mighty are at work to wipe out those who cannot adapt to their hideous imperial culture and inhumane way of life; they blatantly ignore the fact that pain and suffering breeds animosity and hatred.

The crux of matter is this: unless campaign contributions devoted to buying and selling political processes are stopped, we will always encounter these ugly and inhumane actions that are depleted of dignity. There is no responsibility or any trustworthiness left in politicians; it is like playing the game of "Monopoly," where everything goes, since decent playing ethics are mocked and a fair game is impossible. It is sad to say that a surreptitious coup d'état is taking place under cover of corporate anonymity, slowly usurping the freedom-oriented values that we hold sacred and are proud of—all in the name of power. A traditionally exerted dictatorship by an autocratic regime or a monarch is not the case in western societies, but rather an inconspicuous force of corporate might and influence known as plutocracy has sharply influenced many governments. This hold on power by the wealthy affects the culture of geopolitical, economic and social agendas, and thus is able to construct financially tyrannical empires, putting a chokehold on critical matters vital to public and human welfare. Not learning from the historical effect of previous empires of force, they have hollowed themselves on the inside. Such inhumane behaviors have always boomeranged back to the demented culprits and the sadistic violators making them.

Franklin D. Roosevelt once stated, "We had to struggle with the old enemies of peace—business and financial monopoly, speculation, reckless banking, class antagonism, sectionalism, war profiteering. They had begun to consider the Government of the United States as a mere appendage to their own affairs. We know now that Government by organized money is just as dangerous as Government by organized mob. Never before in all our history have these forces been as united against one candidate as they stand today. They are unanimous in their hate for me—and I welcome their hatred." Jesus of Nazareth said: "It is easier for a camel to go through the eye of a needle than for a rich person to enter the kingdom of God." I am sure the prophet of God knew how the concentration of too much wealth in one's hand can be so devastatingly damaging, and that the misallocation of resources can cause prevalent disaster for humanity.

We need to take our blinders off and revere every human being's birthright, to cherish living, and to let everyone dance to the sacred music of life. Stop talking about desolation and, Armageddon, and stall other warmongering ideas serving those in charge of industrial growth for profit. Replace them with the culture of solidarity, love, brotherhood, courage, empathy, and generosity, and let the good in humanity ripen to benefit mankind. We ought to realize that the controversial issues facing humanity are not perpetual illusions, they are a menace to society caused by the financial despots and multinational corporations to maintain the status quo. These entities should be faced head on, not through violence, but with collective reasoning, wit, and in the name of decency, civil liberty, good conscience, and the law. Roosevelt further argued that the economic world had altered since the American founding and the early 19th century. He called for that the country confronted large monopolistic corporations whose power was too great. The suffering of the poor was the result. Unlike in Mill's time, in the new century, we witness a "tyranny of minorities." Namely the wealthy few and their representatives. In respond we need a new version of the three R, s: reform, regulation, and redistribution. Roosevelt named his plan the Square Deal and the New Nationalism. In spite of the fact that he persisted that he was no foeman of capitalism, his rhetoric insinuated some principle limitation on capitalism. We must remove unearned possessions and privileges and promote practical equality of opportunity. He went on to say that property rights are good but only when they benefit society.

Let's look the anatomy of self-alienation. Because the system is an individualistic system, only individuals and aggregations of individuals exist. In order for a person to survive, one's moral mission must be to act in self-interest, conditioned by a Napoleon complex and/or Genghis Khan Mentality to operate under the premises of sociopathic behavior. Because the entire setting is culturally misdirected, economically ruthless and UN-justifying behavior is devised by ruling elites, where social norms are led toward reinforcing and strengthening the pillars of the entire system to enormously benefit the mega-rich. Hence, one must act antisocially toward one's co-workers, consumers and competitors, deviating from what is just and moral so that he will be able to keep up with the pressure of wrongful competition and ultimately avoid failure. In this, one is pushed into an irrational ebullience, where objectives to reach monetary goals and financial successes are the emphasis. Bear in mind that in the context of productivity, the ownership of the social means of production is a key factor in classifying various economic systems.

Contemporary age corporations own land, factories, raw materials, natural resources, labor, facilities, machinery, tools, infrastructural capital and natural capital, as well as the means of distribution. Through the instrument of labor (mainly division of labor) and acting on the means of production, goods are generated. The current mode of production insists on outsourcing jobs to acquire cheap labor and inexpensive raw materials, annexing poor nations' natural resources and finding safe havens to avoid paying billions in taxes. Advanced exploitive techniques such as *division of labor* and *economies of scale* are utilized because of "unjustified and unfair allocation of resources. Huge interest revenues are compounded and imposed on debtors that accumulate an astronomical rate of return. These are the reasons, among many others, for so much surplus value and wealth creation for the mega-rich. We are turning workers into objects, treating them as part of the machinery, and estranging them from true self.

Look, let's face it. There are always going to be inequalities, but forcing the actual producer of wealth—the workers, the middle class—into austerity, exerting a stagnation of wages that co-exists with a sometimes compounding inflationary rate. This is a serious problem and the dung of the devil, since it exterminates even the very basic standard of living and the masses' livelihood and hope for survival. Liberating capital and unleashing investments with no proper management and professional supervision, policies that are exhausted from any moral fiber and depleted from any humane intention, declaring war on nature and its resources, putting the very essence of life at grave risk of eradication—this is what Neoliberalism economics is all about. It pushes the inhabitants to their limits, resulting in the peoples' cry for mercy—all to no avail.

The system does not leave one with much choice, since it controls geopolitical narratives and social and economic agendas. One perhaps is not by nature a sociopathic character, but is forced to comply with the forms of behavior constructed into the system if one intends to function and survive. It alienates and segregates individuals from others, because communal work and/or cooperative actions are not encouraged; the system ignores the fact that we are cooperative beings and must collectively evolve based on our human needs and related challenges with nature, not according to concentration of wealth just for the few. The system is literally destroying planet Earth and its inhabitants.

The system alienates us from nature. We have lost our connection with Mother Nature and her bio-diversity and ecosystem, from plants and animals that are becoming endangered and abstract species—so many have already become extinct. We behave with no conscience and cannot fathom how the so-called modern societies have lost touch with the vitality and the importance of human interconnectedness and our necessary sustenance from planet Earth. The corporations' insatiable behavior in producing unfriendly products has polluted the air, contaminated the water and has poisoned our food so that almost everyone is at grave risk of related health hazards.

It sure alienates one from God, because people with too much wealth and power *play* God. History is witness to mean-spirited rulers that were the embodiment of ruthlessness and tyrannical behavior because of their overwhelming wealth, power and influence. It must sink in that no mortal should be trusted with too much power; balance needs to be restored and play a decisive role in society if we are to halt carnage and the extermination of the weak. Sadly, transnational corporations with astronomical digits of wealth and too much power and influence act neurotic and exploit Earth's natural resources to the point of exhaustion with impunity. The corporate world pushes consumerism when no good products have flooded the markets and homes that are unhealthy. So many consumers are addicted to hoarding products they do not need, and thus bear their ill consequences with no remorse. We are deficit in public goods, since a viable education and good schooling remains unavailable for the average person. These individuals also have to bear the strain of no housing, no health, no reliable infrastructure and roads, no efficient public transportation, and inadequate employment. This has since made the private sector opulent and the public sector squalid. In addition, the judicial system for the poor is anything but fair and just—it is a flagrant abuse of human rights.

Many governments behave like foot soldiers to execute the toxic demands of the .01 percent of the 1 percent of the global population that owns 99 percent of the wealth of the world that we live in, where about 50 percent of the global inhabitants have no wealth. I wonder how such appalling systems can in good faith claim God, and claim not to be so far apart from the almighty. The cynical conduct of the corporations and their unlimited buying power and influence have bought so many undignified powerful souls to act as accessories and puppets on their behalf, creating a plutocratic regime that acts against the will of the people and its republic. They have gained so much wealth and power, both beyond comprehension, and this has led to the narrow-minded orchestration of objectives set to only maximize profit no matter the cost.

One global financial malignancy out of many is that multi-national corporations are exploiting taxes and evading paying billions because of flimsy laws and regulations handmade for the mega-rich, who can afford charlatan accountants and unscrupulous attorneys to manipulate loopholes. If these loopholes are corrected and properly enforced (which they have not been, to date), they can decisively mitigate these concerns, bring some balance to the world economy, and narrow the wide gap between the super-rich and the rest of society a bit. It is mind-boggling to know that governments can make the common man pay taxes to the last penny, but turn a blind eye to the trillions of dollars in unpaid taxes of financial tyrants and moguls of the world that we live in. Why should corporations have the freedom to destroy the world? They create extremely high volumes of carbon monoxide emissions and do not pay a single dollar in taxes. If the fossil fuel industries were taxed, it would motivate them to move toward renewable energy alternatives, since we have the technology to manufacture wind power, solar power, hydroelectric power, as well as other safe and efficient options.

Both mass media and the entire propaganda machine are biased and owned by the richest one percent. They are unquestionably rigged, they perpetuate misrepresentation, which makes it very difficult for so many to make the right choice. Our tunnel vision does not allow us to see other real-value systems and sensible opportunities available that can help everyone to prosper and put a stop to endless growth fueled by greed and the insatiable production of unfriendly products. The impetus for a whole new system will occur since people are willing to listen and are becoming aware of what is actually transpiring around them.

The economic strategies of the transnational corporations are further unleashed as they corroborate in a global market economy where the mechanics of market interactions are unimaginably demanding. Only the multinational corporations can identify with and manage these insurmountable daily transactions that exceed several trillions of dollars (blatantly taking place electronically), while too many others are unable to live their lives, so indignant with poverty, making the alternative of death a blessing for millions.

Obviously the answer is not violent revolution or a dictatorial system of any kind, either socialism or communism. No system can stop its inhabitants from dreaming, from asking why and believing in reason, from creativity, from hoping, from believing in God, from having faith, and from the pursuit of happiness. People cannot be stopped from seeking justice and liberty, from desire, from wanting to make a better life, from seeking security, from having peace, from inspiring, from imagining, or from worshiping beauty. Likewise: from behaving rational; from being able to choose; from caring and active philanthropy; from loving; from believing in themselves; from their civil and property rights; from acting compassionate and with empathy; from living with dignity, and so many other vital issues ingratiated with human spirit.

No system can turn human beings into robots. People will eventually wake up, as if they had a bad dream, because human feelings are scared and extremely potent. It is a phenomenon that is linked to both the heavens above and to the terrestrial realm, and this is no joke. For instance when one loses a loved one, one is mentally and emotionally affected for the rest of one's life, or when one's trust is betrayed, or if victimized by an abusive relative, one will always remember the mental anguish and sentimental hurt. Human emotions and feelings are the embodiment of heaven and hell promised; they are very case-specific and must be dealt with skillfully and convincingly. When human beings are emotionally hurt, betrayed or denied love or are abused, there is always potential for violence, and often hell breaks loose.

Any system of government that dehumanizes people and behaves boorish towards its civilians, alienating them from their freedom, livelihood, and happiness, will eventually be annihilated no matter at what height of power or might they seem to be. To prove that, all one needs to do is to pay attention to the history of the Ottoman Empire supported by their German allies, which caused the first genocide of the twentieth century in 1915 against the Armenians (or Roman Empire), Greek Empire, Persian Empire, Chinese and Mongolian Empires, Egyptian Empire and so many other mighty Empires of the past. They perished because of their horrific and inhumane actions. We need to bear in mind that crimes against humanity and malevolent behaviors against mankind can come in many shapes and forms; the worst are the wicked financial planning and premeditated economic coups d'état against many societies, which can strip an entire nation from having the right to live—to depleting them of the basic amenities to survive.

Instead we need an educated government with a heart, one that encourages moderation and balance, believes in due process of law, and is accountable enough to implement the rule of the land with no prejudices. There are many humane economic alternatives to the brutal, heartless system of mega corporations that are much more justified and feasible like the system of co-ops, or a social democratic system of governing. Humanism is restored and citizens are ensured of basic necessities instead of becoming victims of horrifying financial breakdowns due to sudden economic depression or other back-breaking financial maladies facing so many. But any free society with a viable economic system should rely heavily on a meaningful democratic infrastructure where popular democratic institutions are strengthened and can genuinely promote democratic values with decent principles.

Most of all, every nation needs a God-fearing panel of experts, some type of national council that is superbly educated and understands the gravity of their responsibility. The council must embody unwavering virtue, high moral competency, and legislatively savviness, and include some type of philosopher king-like characters. They must also maintain professionalism within the vicinity of the law to oversee the government's transparencies and ensure the clean functioning of its regulatory bodies. In short, they must make certain that the rules of republic are unquestionably implemented so that a more egalitarian society is established. It is also true that any nation with a corrupt and disintegrating economic system will produce vast numbers of unemployed and a financial depression that can lead to social unrest and upheaval, making the entire society vulnerable to militarism, repression and fascism.

And yes, historically speaking violence has played a major role in people's last resort for changing undesirable and inhumane regimes. However, we live in the twenty-first century. Nothing short of the power of syllogism, or behaving irresponsibly, irrationally or in a non-peaceful manner should exemplify savagery and barbarism. If an undemocratic situation persists, dissidents must encourage peaceful civil disobedience, constitute more unions, and organize non-violent strikes where Mahatma Gandhi's and Martin Luther King's mentalities or Mandala's way of defiance can become the norm and the key against corporate greed. Many oppressed nations have been justified in using defiance to indemnify lives through incessant and peaceful resistance, not limited to occasional and fragmented communal activities, but also occurring in large scale. Why do the masses' struggles need to be peaceful and sane? It is because human lives are precious and must not be wasted, no matter which side one is on.

The truth is that we all have both good and evil within us; the test is to purge and redeem one's self iniquity and leave this world better than when one finds it. Besides, how do we know what virtue is without knowing evil? How can anyone truly value love and compassion without knowing hate and animosity? How can we value safety without understanding hazard; how can we identify with health without knowing sickness; and how can we value life without noticing the shadow of death lurking about, closer than our aorta to our neck? Zoroastrian faith believes there is good and evil in all of us, and we must choose goodness over evil. Since the problems of this world are manmade, they must be resolved by the goodness within man.

It seems we can become enlightened by experiencing ignorance, and can perceive light by experiencing darkness. How can we realize the value for anything without discerning its opposite? As weird as it seems, it is a blessing to vividly understand the wicked forces of nature, including the ills of human nature, since without them, no meaning to positive life-driven objectives can be possible. Where energy-driven consciousness permeates into the spirit of evil and awakens the very soul holding it hostage, there is always hope for the worst offender of them all to identify with his higher self, and to understand that it is all about passing life's challenging tests. It is odd but true that evil drives us to be good. Yes, we do need to pay attention to neuroscience and other medical-related fields that indicate an under-developed lobe in some people's brains when growing up that is in need of early detection and professional therapy. The overwhelming evidence clearly indicates the need to coalesce and unite together to efficiently benefit from collective intelligence and consciousness, to insightfully challenge the difficulties of life facing us. The way to my country and my God, and your country and your God, is a problematic way, an incomplete phase of our lives, a fragmented thought which is in need of wise and constructive mending. Humanity is gifted with intelligence, scared emotions and action. Let's invest in and capitalize on them so that no one is left behind. This is the way to the heaven promised.

Essay 7
Attention Deficit Disorder

Let's try to understand why things are the way they are. If they were to function differently, would we still be able to carry on with our lives as we do? Let's imagine that if we had to breathe voluntarily, that this ability wasn't on autopilot. It would be impossible to live! We are bound to forget because we have to put all our energy into our busy life styles, which can make us avoid remembering the very essence of our existence, breathing. Most of the time it seems we are hibernating and essentially numb to our breathing; in the new scenario, breathing is suddenly questionable. This would not be so if we were active in our breathing. So why are we not aware of it? Je Gampopa (1079-1153), on the miracle of breathing, said, "There are many things which harm life. As life is more unstable than an air bubble in water, it is a wonder that in-breaths turn into out-breaths and that one wakes up from sleep."

If we had the choice to know what happens after we die, and if it became apparent that there is a better life out there, do you think it would be possible to experience life as we know it? If this were the case, then everyone would want to commit suicide, with no motivation to face anxiety and confront pain and suffering. One would simply go where he or she is to be happier and better off. It would not give the evolutionary cycle the chance to take its natural course as it is meant to be.

Imagine if we were passionately in love at all times. Since time passes in a blink an eye when in love, then naturally no one would want to exit this state of romantic mindset, engulfed with elated feelings and miracle-like emotions. It would make us procrastinate, even forget about our daily chores and vital issues in our lives; it would be almost impossible for anyone to accomplish even a bare minimum of constructive work. This is why balance should be the essence of all that we do, even when referring to moderation in loving.

Imagine if time did not heal our pain, and did not mitigate our suffering when we experience the hurts and tragedies of life's ugliest incidents, which are sometimes heinous beyond human belief. It is only possible to subjugate our grief and gain the ability to overcome it with passing time. Time helps us eventually forget the painful emotions so we can ultimately exit our mourning state of mind, making it possible to carry on with life's journey.

Imagine if we were not afforded the chance to get used to our incremental and gradual changes as we age; this natural process would be sudden and not smoothly integrated over the years the way it has been. It would certainly provoke horror and shock us beyond belief to one day wake up and notice that we have gone old and wrinkly overnight; this would not be practical.

Imagine that we couldn't mature and grow to become enlightened, which enables us to get out of this intoxicating mentality where our only priority is fixated on the material world of sex, wealth, violence, power and influence. The quest for power and influence causes so much agony in the name of business due to a single-track mindset aimed at getting rich. If it were not possible to progress from ignorance to sanity, from fear to love and kindness, and from an anxiety-driven environment to a more relaxed and peaceful world, little things in life wouldn't mean so much; I am afraid they are otherwise taken for granted.

Imagine if we were to live one thousand years, not concerned about our short average life span of seventy to eighty years. What if for this time span we were still stuck in a self-centered state of mind, motivated only by self-interest? We would turn into most savage and despicable creatures, doing beastly wrongs to accumulate enough wealth to last us for so long.

Imagine if we were not logical and flexible enough to justify our pain and suffering, and thus were not able to adapt to the difficulties in our lives or absorb and overcome the obstacles in our way. Such challenging difficulties can help us to become much stronger mentally, spiritually, and physically, just like a tiny seed that needs to push its way up and out from the soil to gradually blossom, eventually to grow into strong and beautiful tree.

Imagine we were not able to feel hunger, thirst, love, sleep, wakefulness or rested. What if we were unable to feel cold or heat, or were not aware of needing empty our bowels or feeling the urge to urinate?

Imagine not feeling the heat when we are literally next to a fire, or not being able to instinctively pull away from the shock of electricity or a very hot stove. Imagine if we needed to sharpen our memory, like winding up a digital clock, every morning before starting our day. Imagine if we could not memorize our everyday to-do lists due to a dysfunctional memory.

Imagine that we could not "imagine." We might then devolve into bunch of blunt and languid creatures. Can you imagine if we all looked the same? Can anyone imagine what it would be like if we all possessed the same fingerprints, or the same DNA? We would all have the same appetites, the same tastes in so many things, and would not be neither diversified nor unique in our talents.

Imagine if we could not cry out in pain and suffering, involuntarily bursting into tears; such action acts as a safety valve to release our internal pressure. Just like so many other natural phenomena in our lives, we take them for granted. Mary Rose Magnay said, "Crying makes you strong-so cry whenever you need it for it can help you relieve the pain from within."

Our smiling face and pleasant laugh vibrates positive energy and kindness to others. Doctors believe it takes twenty-six muscle to smile, while it takes sixty two muscle to frown, so it is a blessing to smile. Our facial expressions reflect all kinds of different information that can be translated and interpreted by other people. Thousands of various messages are intimated by expanding or contracting our facial muscles, which reveal our emotional state of being. One can detect our physical and emotional health, our well-being, our mental state, and how credible we are (or if we can perceive their own credibility); often we take this for granted.

Imagine that we consciously felt the heaviness of our head every day, twenty four hours a day, seven days a week, and the sum total weight of our internal organs, mainly our stomach. Imagine if climate change caused the weather to vacillate between extreme and intolerable degrees of heat and cold. It would be impossible to bear the climate, no matter how advanced we are in manufacturing heating and air-conditioning systems. Millions of other happenings that we are not thinking of on a daily basis are in operation. Consider that the solar system, the sun, the moon, stars, black holes, billions of galaxies, universes, gravity, electromagnetic forces, atomic forces, and other such systems operate with an unbelievable precision and discipline. Imagine if Earth's gravitational force malfunctioned for couple of seconds; the entire cosmos would turn upside-down into state of complete chaos.

Imagine if we could not blink automatically. We blink about twenty-five to twenty-seven times a minute while we are awake; tear glands in the outside corners of our eyes are constantly making tears, and when we blink, our eyelids wipe them away so that the front surfaces of our eyes are kept clean and moist. Blinking is also managed by a reflex called automatic nerve action, which makes our eyes blink regularly. Instinctual blinking closes our eyelids when something is about to strike the face, which protects the eye. So why do we blink so often? New scientific research shows that our brain actually enters a momentary state of alertness and wakeful rest when we blink, which scientists believe allows us to focus better each time it happens.

Should we not notice our inner inquisitiveness when it seeks to understand what befuddles us and urges us to find a solution? Eye-opening revelations do not typically present themselves vociferously, but very softly tap one on the shoulder with breakthrough ideas. Sometimes life-changing and positive vibration radiates into our life that matters decisively, but then, so many take this for granted. Epiphany and brainstorming can sometimes allow us to ascend and appreciate higher realms of knowledge that open the doors to sometimes very enigmatic situations. We need to awaken to the things we take for granted, since the more acquainted we become and spend time with the things around us—even the most beautiful and wonderful things—the more they become unnoticed to us. That is why we often take the beauty of this world for granted: the flowers, the trees, the birds and the bees, full moon, the stars and the clouds, the sunshine and fresh air, a friendly and kind smile, and seeing our loved ones in good health. Because we notice them so often, we truly "see" them less and less, even those we love so much.

Imagine if we could feel food and the water descending through our digestive systems. Imagine feeling it move through the gut by peristalsis, which involves successive waves of involuntary contractions passing along the wall of a hollow muscular structure such as the esophagus or intestine and progressing the contents onward. In approximately twelve to fourteen hours, our stomach contents become digested for the purpose of extracting the nutrients needed to adequately nourish our bodies. What if we could feel and hear the food growling, gradually and noisily descending—paradoxical to what we really experience, which is comfort and the satisfaction of our hunger?

Some perhaps believe that turning and tossing while sleeping at night leads to a disruptive sleep. Not so, since there are many scientific and biological reasons behind this phenomenon. Dr. Harriet Hiscock, a pediatric sleep specialist at the <u>Royal Children's Hospital</u> Melbourne, says that, "No one that I'm aware of has specifically researched this." Rolling over in bed is something we take for granted, yet it appears we know very little about this basic human movement. Babies start to roll at about four months, says Hiscock. She states that before this time, "they don't have the coordination to do it and they are simply not strong enough." Furthermore, "There's a big innate drive so that they learn to roll so they can get on all fours and start to crawl," she says, adding that rolling over is a "developmental milestone."

She thinks that rolling over during sleep for adults and children is simply a matter of getting comfortable. "If you just lie in the same position all night you'd probably get stiff joints, and problems with the skin," she suggests. Dr. Peter Roessler, a fellow of the <u>Australian and New Zealand College of Anesthetists</u>, agrees. "I think movement while we are asleep is a protective mechanism to prevent problems developing from prolonged pressure—such as reduced blood flow to certain parts of the skin," he says. When patients are paralyzed for a long time, for example in intensive care, they need to be turned regularly to prevent pressure sores, he adds. They believe that unpleasant stimuli from pressure on pain receptors (called nociceptors) initiates a coordinated rolling over response, and this can happen whether we are asleep, or simply lying awake in bed. "We've all experienced this when sitting in one position. We can tolerate it for a certain length of time and then we have to move. I suspect it's probably a similar sort of response even when we are asleep." He says that "The signals from the nociceptors (a pain sense organ) would travel up the back of the spinal cord to the brain, possibly to the reticular (connective tissue with collagen) activating system which is important in sleep and wakening. Then signals to make movement happen would travel down tracts in the front portion of the spinal cord and go out to the muscles. People under anesthesia can't roll over because their sensory signals are suppressed, muscle power is diminished and brain activity can't be coordinated," he adds. "And the most common reason for someone turning over in their sleep is probably their spouse nudging them to stop them snoring," he laughs.

So how conscious do you need to be to detect these signals? Hiscock thinks rolling mainly occurs during deep sleep. "As we go through the night we cycle through alternating phases of light and deep sleep," she says. "Rolling and other movements are not going to happen in the light sleep phase known as rapid eye movement sleep (or REM sleep). When we are in [REM] sleep we tend to dream and our body is semi-paralyzed, so we can't roll over. We think that's to stop us acting out our dreams," she says. According to Dr. Chris Seton, a child sleep physician at The Children's Hospital Westmead in Sydney, during deep non-REM sleep, the brain has mini 'arousals' every six to eight minutes when the sleeper becomes more awake. "Arousals are a normal phenomenon, and everyone does it," says Seton. He says arousals are almost invariably associated with some body movement—maybe just kicking out a leg, or sometimes, rolling over. "What we know is that if you have an arousal at the same time for instance, that somebody comes into your bedroom, you will wake up. But if you have an arousal and there's no environmental threat happening then you just go back to sleep. It's like an alerting mechanism — a monitor," he says. "The arousal is a protective mechanism. The movement doesn't do anything—it's an ancillary event." Interestingly he says that boys move more than girls when they have an arousal. "The evolutionary basis of that is that the men were the protectors," he says, "so they would need to be ready to fight off an intruder — perhaps a tiger in the cave." Now that would be a reason to move!

To recap, Drs. Harriet Hiscock, Peter Roessler, and Chris Seton were interviewed by Clare Pain. According to these prominent specialists, when we are in [REM] sleep and we tend to dream, our body is semi-paralyzed, but then imagine if we were not half-paralyzed; logic should tell us that we would want to play our dreams out—even the wild ones—which would put us in danger due to such active movement while sleeping.

Another thing we take for granted? Saliva. When we salivate, six groups of cells known as salivary glands make salvia. Through ducts, the glands exude the saliva into the mouth. Saliva is mostly water. It does contain a lot of enzymes, which are special chemicals that protect the mouth against infection and help to soften food for digestion. Saliva also keeps the mouth from drying out. Glands produce more saliva when food is in the mouth. Besides helping to break down food, saliva lubricates the throat, which makes swallowing food easier. Saliva is very important to our oral hygiene since it helps one taste, chew and swallow food. It fights germs in the <u>mouth</u> and prevents <u>bad breath</u>, has proteins and minerals which protect <u>tooth enamel</u> and prevent gum disease and <u>tooth</u> decay, keeps the <u>mouth</u> moist and comfortable, and helps keep dentures tightly in place.

There are thousands of awesome and very intricate activities which take place in our body automatically, without any discomfort to us, and each and every occurrence happens for a sensible reason. This happens in nature as well, and we are an essential part of that. We take this marvel of supreme design for granted, when we should try more to emulate and respect it in ourselves and nature, to let it resonate into our lives. The point is that we are all energetic beings connected to the cosmos through our conscious awareness and our awakened mind. This makes us all a single entity, inseparable from one another and nature. We ought to know that all things in nature have just the right reason to operate as they are programmed. When we choose to go beyond our limits in dealing with Mother Nature, the planet Earth and each other, all sorts of mayhem and discord occurs that affects all of us for the worse.

The information available to us is in the form of energy that enters our senses, which gives us the unique potential to identify with each other through our happiness and our sadness, through our pain and suffering, through our hopes and desires, and through our love for humanity even though we may dislike others. This is what makes us the group animals that we are, able to conquer the puzzles of our world collectively—to reach stars and to explore other planets. But before we get there, we must first give priority to peace, to bettering our planet Earth and in striving for collective happiness.

We should leave behind our material addictions and stop religiously perusing wealth, as such pursuits lead to the unfair allocation of resources, ultimately ending in human disaster. This excessive consumption has turned into a compulsive disorder, making human life miserable. Our emotional fitness and psychological strengths must come into accord with nature; balance must be restored for humanity to survive. We must let go of this delusional state of mind and give our lives the reality they deserve, in order to enjoy life as it is meant to be. We need to break out of this attention deficit disorder and hyperactively negligent mode of not listening to nature. What I am saying is that we must make our thought process, behaviors, deeds, and actions compatible with the way nature operates, that is, always in tune with generosity and balance.

We have the potential to be hugely compassionate; when a speck of life energy is ingrained with kindness, love, and pity that permeates every animated being, it can become a very potent force to contend with indeed. Often, however, we are blind, and deliberately choose not to utilize or act upon these heavenly emotions to create a better world. Imagine if we did not have the urge to mingle and to love, if we were not sociable creatures or created as group animals. Without a sense of belonging we would be forever lost and discontent, which would put our entire existence at risk. We repel and reject this colossal miracle of human kindness and love when we adhere to violence, and regrettably so. Perhaps it is time to stop being so proud of our actions of dismay toward each other and let our true human attributes of empathy and compassion take over. Perhaps now is the time to wake up and remedy our attention deficit disorder.

Essay 8

Human Nature versus Nurture

Some human traits are mandatory and essential to our survival: we must breathe, eat, drink, sleep, copulate, rest, work, and since by nature we are group creatures, it is vital that we often socialize. These innate characteristics are imposed by nature at the time of conception and further develop as we grow into a fetus and continuing after we are born. If we are forced to halt our instinctual properties we will no doubt perish. The human limbic and neurological systems, respiratory system, cardiovascular system, digestive system, lymphatic system, musculoskeletal system, reproductive system, circulatory system, biliary system, our endocrine system, integumentary system, and other bodily systems—all of these are on auto pilot as long as we remain in an environment that supports them. Obviously good nutrition, rest and good food, a clean environment with fresh air and water, proper sanitation, appropriate rest and decent sleep, adequate exercise and movement, meditation, pleasant copulation, and going through life with a positive attitude with smiles on our faces, are very decisive in our well-being.

Nature and heredity (the transmission of genetic characteristics) play a large role in our health, including whether we have good health, a shortened life span, and in some fashion, how our human offspring look and behave. But this should not be mysterious or in any way mislead us into believing that nurture and nature are separate and not integrated. Our nature feeds on how we are nurtured and our welfare is certainly the byproduct of how we are raised and how we fare in life. "Genes play an absolutely pivotal role in human health," states Dr. David Perl mutter, renowned neurologist and president of the Perl mutter Health Center in Florida, "but 99 percent of the genes and 99 percent of DNA in our body are not ours." He then explains that "the majority of genes in the body belong to the micro biota in our guts—and they have a big influence on how we age. The National Institute of Health's Human Micro biome Project reveals that "one of the most revolutionary areas of health research has to do with our Micro biome, that collection of tiny organisms living in and on our body that are essential partners in good health." According to the Human Micro biome Project, these microbes "produce some vitamins that we do not have the genes to make, break down our food to extract nutrients we need to survive, teach our immune systems how to recognize dangerous invaders, and even produce helpful anti-inflammatory compounds that fight off other disease-causing microbes." Perl mutter refers to a 2015 study in the open-access, peer-reviewed *Journal of Neuro-inflammation* that indicates that "chronic inflammation of the gut causes a decrease in the formation of new cells in the hippocampus, a process that normally continues throughout adulthood and is linked to cognition and mood." Another crucial factor is that human's do what is in their nature, which is to stay connected, since no man is a remote island.

In 2014, University of Chicago psychologist John Cacioppo discovered that "feeling extreme loneliness can increase an older person's chances of premature death by 14 percent." The study also referenced a 2014 meta-analysis which found that "loneliness has twice the impact on early death as obesity does." Many studies have revealed that feeling connected socially and emotionally and enjoying a sense of belonging can actually reduce the biomarkers of a stressful life and improve one's overall health. If combined with a good immune support system, such feelings can go a long way toward lowering inflammation, which affects one's gene expression, hormonal balance, and energy levels for the better. Scientists believe that epigenetic changes are influenced by nature. That is, chemical changes involved in turning on or off certain genes are triggered faster than the portions of the DNA code that are relatively fixed. An epigenetic change instigated by environmental conditions may be reversed when environmental conditions alter again.

In his best-selling book, *The Blue Zones: Lessons for Living Longer From the People Who've Lived the Longest*, National Geographic explorer Dan Buettner designated a strong sense of belonging and community interaction as one of the top factors influencing not only one's chances of living to 100, but of living to 100 as a reasonably healthy and happy person. In the online health and fitness magazine *Experience Life* (Nov 2015), Kristin Ohlson states in her article *The Big Picture: 5 Fundamentals of Lifetime Health,* "our cells replace themselves throughout our lives, and the raw materials for these new cells come from our diets." She carries on to say that "the best source for most nutrients is good food-fresh vegetables, fruits, nuts, seeds, and legumes grown in healthy soil and water without chemicals and synthetic additives, wild-caught cold water fish; and meat, eggs, and other products raised on pasture." Some experts in nutrition still claim that even the best diet can potentially leave out some nutrients, so they suggest taking supplements to amplify the body's resiliency against aging. They recommend:

- well-balanced multivitamin for micronutrients
- a high- potency probiotic like yogurt, kefir, Korean kimchee, or kombucha
- The consumption of food with fiber, including onion, garlic, raw dandelion greens, banana, and Jerusalem artichokes. vitamin D to support immune system function
- omega-3 and fish oil capsules for essential fatty acids that helps against inflammation and support brain health
- turmeric to help and protect against inflammation
- NAC (N-acetyl cysteine) to help support detoxification
- resveratrol for mitochondrial support, and
- CoQ10 to slow cardiovascular support.

Understanding that our brain and our nervous system, our memory and senses, our thoughts and emotions, and the ability to behave compassionately and act with empathy is so very important. Without this understanding we will operate like zombies, cut off from the reality of our world in every practical and meaningful way. It is very much necessary that we protect and boost the power of the brain nutritionally, by taking in foods that will help us strengthen our memory power and the overall health of our brains and nervous systems. This has been well assessed by the medical community and dietitians over time; prominent brain surgeons, psychiatrics and neurological authorities have concluded that refined sugar, bleached flour, saturated fats (bacon, red meat, dairy products, milk and chesses, pizza, egg yolks, etc.), salt, processed foods, sweeteners, preservatives, artificial additives, hormones, and artificial coloring, sodas, MSG, gluten, antibiotic-driven foods, and trans fat in some foods will damage not only our brains and our nervous systems, but also trigger unheard-of diseases that menace our health and threaten our very existence.

Losing our memory and the power of our thoughts is not a joke, it will clearly separate us from the rest of the world. Alcohol and drugs, prescription pharmaceuticals, cigarette smoking, and eating too much fried food and red meat will also expedite the deterioration of our health and memory loss. The experts and medical authorities believe that these horrifying foods and drinks can damage billions of links and connective micro tissues, also known as "synopses" in the brain, that play a very important role by interactively communicating with billions of other cells to create dynamic thoughts. For example, the principal use of azodicarbonamide is in the production of foamed plastic as a blowing agent. It is also utilized in other plastics, and in synthetic leather. It aids in the manufacture of <u>vinyl (PVC)</u> foam, where it plays a role in the formation of air bubbles by breaking down into gas at high temperature. Azodicarbonamide is a killing agent that is utilized as a food additive to bleach flour and also as a dough conditioner. It has been banned in Europe for any use in food products, since it leads to many health hazards including leaky gut syndrome, fatigue, bloating, cramps and indigestion, skin rashes, and brain fogging or difficulty to concentrate. Unfortunately the corporate takeover of many governments has led to distortion of the truth and a misconception that genes are perhaps magically implanted in us from out of the blue. We need to be ever-conscious of the essence of every experience, and understand that consciousness is a matrix processed at a different levels. As our collective knowledge and wisdom rises there are more chances to win against greed and wrongful accumulation of wealth at the expenses of people's lives.

Medical communities also believe that lack of proper sleep and lack of exercise are also contributing factors in the deterioration of our vital bodily organs, especially our brains and nervous systems. A host of other conditions are brought on by profit-driven motives and corporate greed. Examples include: impotency, high blood pressures, heart attacks, strokes, kidney (renal) diseases, lung problems, high triglycerides, high cholesterol, obesity, many types of cancer (brain cancer, lung cancer, colon cancer, prostate cancer, breast cancer, pancreatic cancer, leukemia), skin and auto immune diseases, Alzheimer disease, Parkinson's disease, multiple sclerosis, arthritis, Lou Gehrig's disease (a devastating health problem that attacks the nerves and muscle), tooth decay, and hundreds of other problems facing humanity. Our lack of knowledge and ignorance in not protecting ourselves against these types of poisonous foods and environments, are also contributing factors. Because they contain high levels of iron, copper, and other minerals, it is also believed that these foods cause oxidization, a process in the human body that damages cell membranes and other structures, including cellular proteins, lipids and DNA. This causes damage to many of the linkages and connections to our brain cells, triggering memory loss.

It is so very important to protect ourselves from these foods, and to consume organic, leafy green vegetables, vegetables with different varieties of coloring and freshness, fruits of many sorts, nuts, and an assortment of beans. Other beneficial foods include whole grain bread and pasta, spices such as curry powder, ginger, red and black pepper, cayenne pepper, cumin, turmeric, coriander, cinnamon, and garlic salt, and other naturally-derived seasonings as most of them have marvelous antioxidant qualities. Finally, drinking purified water will help cleanse your body to promote easy digestion. Remember that any kind of physical exercise will help prevent the brain from shrinking; it is also believed by the medical community and researchers that aerobic exercise actually expands the grey matter in our brains, boosting memory function.

If one cannot stay away from eating meat, then moderation is recommended, consuming only natural grain-fed chicken and grass-fed lamb and beef raised in a stress- and cage- free environment, with no hormonal or antibiotic enhancement or preservatives used in processing. One should also take high quality multivitamins, especially vitamin B12 and B complex for the brain, also vitamins A, C, D, E, and quality fish oil for clarity of mind and good memory. Minerals play an important role as well. Stick to consuming good fats; use healthier oils such as coconut, grape, olive, and almond, and stay away from bad fats and free radicals.

A plant-based diet is loaded with micronutrients, and provides the best nutritional properties for a not only a refreshing memory that will last a long time, but also beautiful hair and skin. You will be free from clogged and plaque-lined arteries that are directly related to strokes and heart disease, impotency, and many other drastic problems. Stay away from cooking in aluminum, copper, and iron pots, pans, and skillets. These metals also introduce poisons into our bodies, causing memory shortages. Use silver cookware instead, as too much iron, copper, aluminum, and other minerals in our blood can cause memory loss and damaged synapses. You do need iron in your body to make hemoglobin, a protein that carries oxygen to your brain, but too much of it will damage your brain, just like bad fat causes plaques in your brain and other vital organs, such as the heart and the reproductive system.

It is not only me who believes this; the medical authorities, dieticians, and other health care providers sincerely believe it as well. You need to be careful not to see the brain as just wrinkly tissue, or a grey fatty organ that performs simple, uniform deeds. It should be understood that it is the most complex and intricate entity on the face of our planet. It is possible for most of our organs to be replaced, but most definitely not our brain. Our brain is constructed from many multifarious and superbly oriented parts, including the thalamus, hypothalamus, hippocampus, prefrontal cortex (the largest part of our brain, for processing thoughts), and the amygdala (responsible for emotions on both sides of our brain, and part of the limbic system), and so many other complex parts to explore. As the forebrain expands and gets bigger over time, additional miracles of our brains are still to be exposed. The way we live can certainly affect our genes and well-being, which gives meaning to the phrase, "knowledge is power."

If our parents, and to a certain extent our predecessors, were caught in a web of uncertainty, dealing with family violence and anxiety, stress, malnutrition, perhaps drug- and alcohol-related situations, or other kinds of financial, social, and cultural issues, then rest assured genes will be influenced and babies will be born with a host of problems. This holds true from the time our forefathers lived in caves and dealt with dangerous animals. They endured the harshest of environments, from the deep jungles of the Amazon, Africa, and Asia, to treacherous mountains, deserts, sand storms and dry lands, and along the edges of rivers, and oceans. Because they had to constantly deal with the hazards of their atmosphere, including marshes, quicksand, swamps, tsunamis, and other rough terrain and undesirable places, we eventually entered into a more civilized way of life, able to harness nature to better serve humanity.

Our genes definitely had to be influenced by how we lived back then, when adrenaline, known as the "fight or flight hormone," had to have been activated several times a day due to the challenges inherent in survival and just staying alive. They did not know where their next meal would come from, and were constantly dealing with the fear of the unknown when thunder, lightning, storms, earthquakes, and other sudden and unexpected perils were upon them. These settings and way of life were dictated by nature. How our forefathers were treated and lived must have affected their genes. It is nice not to be fooled into believing that genes and hereditary traits appear by magic, "from thin air," or out of nowhere. We are the products of how we live our lives, and certainly living by ghetto-type standards, including a comparable upbringing, would not breed healthy genes. No, I am not saying we are condemned to live in misery, or are cursed to produce not-so-desirable babies. We do have the choice to change our lives, and to drastically alter our genes for the better—even to a rating of excellence, in which one can overcome one's difficult life and improve it to a point where he or she could live happily ever after.

Let's assume we retrieve time from the past, and bring the Stone Age back—that we are literally living in this time period. Of course to do this we must subtract our technologies and advancements, and further deduct all of the amnesties, mental progress, and the comfort that many enjoy in the present era. In other words, if we had to live a caveman's life; can anyone imagine that we would survive the everyday perils of our surroundings? The genes and attributes we carry are the byproducts and the biomarkers of today's modern life style. Our so-called hereditary genes are no longer equipped with what they need to survive within the Stone Age mentality.

We can even affect biological aging for the better, securing a good metabolism, fat-burning capabilities, weight loss, healthy and strong lean muscles, radiant and clear skin, robust energy levels, and an insatiable sex drive. This can be very satisfying, that is, if we can manage to combine these things with a life with no undue distress, one that is not congested with pressures and stress-related issues. This recipe is the secret to a prosperous mentality, spiritual and physical health, and the ability to enjoy a good and healthy life. These biological and inherited characteristics by which our biomarkers and traits are automatically shaped are hard-wired into our genes for survival. We would become less than expected if our seed is planted but not well maintained and appropriately attended to. Just like a flower that needs water, sunshine, nutritious soil, and proper weed trimming, it must not be outside our realm of possibility to ensure that we are well nurtured and maintain ourselves in a loving and caring environment. This will allow nature to meet, and even go beyond, our expectations.

In a study at the University of Utah, researchers showed, in the study "Nurturing Behavior in Rats" that rat pups who receive high or low nurturing from their mothers develop epigenetic differences that affect their response to stress later in life[1]. When the female pups become mothers themselves, the ones that received high quality care become high-nurturing mothers, and the ones that received low quality care become low-nurturing mothers. The nurturing behavior itself transmits epigenetic information into the pups' DNA, without passing through egg or sperm. It is also believed that epigenetic inheritance is a nonconformist finding, it contests the idea that inheritance occurs only through the DNA code that is transmitted from parent to offspring. It shows that a parent's experiences, in the form of epigenetic tags, can be passed down to future generations. The first step is nurturing our mind and spirit, which is accomplished through education and training, gaining intelligence, and ultimately, wisdom. One should start developing positive and virtuous behaviors early on. It all has to do with good conscience and moral characteristics, as well as the acquisition of good knowledge and quality learning. It is about civility and love, compassion, devotion, and recognizing our divine natures. It deals with sacrifice and being selfless, kind, considerate, polite, and respectful, and acquiring peaceful behaviors. It includes feeling sad and melancholy when others are in bondage, and not free.

---

[1]   http://learn.genetics.utah.edu/content/epigenetics/rats/ -

It is about being mindful of people's pain and the suffering of others; it is about substantiating and manifesting our celestial and angelic behaviors and actions, to save others in need. It is about giving priority to those who are desperate for the most basic needs to survive.

It is about wisdom, tutelage, awareness, sacrifice and caring. There is a very fine line between these two, since nature and nurture are enmeshed within them. The latter demands much more attention, such as constructive and vast resources, and ample opportunity to lay a strong foundation to grow and to be fruitful.

Nurture should truly be invested in and paid sincere attention to, otherwise it will disturb the optimal balance and push us toward our animal drives. Our instincts and lower self can take over, leading to beastly behavior and acting on impulse, resulting in a stringently ignorant state of mind. In this environment, we become savage and selfish enough to condone destruction and violence, up to and including annihilation. Some of this trouble is already happening; this should be transparent to the naked eye. We must insist on a violence-free world; if not, there will be ill consequences—not only for those who live it, but also most definitely for newcomers and the next generation. It is a matter of urgency for some of these plagues to be remedied soon and corrected with all possible human might. We must learn how know now; before it is too late. Acting indifferent toward these catastrophes and inhumane actions taken by the bullies of the world is devastating to human society as a whole.

What is clear about our lives and our human natures, and the way we are nurtured and nourished, is that we are all conflated and originate from the same source. We must, therefore, obey the laws of nature if we are to survive. No matter how advanced and industrialized we are, even with all of our technological might, we will be doomed to extinction if forced to stray from the laws of the universe and our rightful place within nature. The manufacture of genetically engineered foods and processed products does sustain us in the short run. But surely this is our ticket to a very unhealthy and destructive life as we are clearly already experiencing. Once more, it is an undeniable fact that we are all interconnected and must act like it, there is just no way around it. We ought to swallow our pride and reject the sense of narcissism, realizing the power within as compared to the power over each other, and vowing not to destroy the only habitat that we have—our planet Earth. Confucius said, "He who wishes to secure the good of others, has already secured his own." Hence, a concerted effort is globally urgent to restore the goodness in both our lives and nature.

We have the potential to be nurtured from nature's plentiful goodness and hence we should respect the sacredness of Mother Nature in a humanistic way. Therefore we need to constructively manage and capitalize upon our gifts from nature by clearly standing at the pinnacle of humanity, far away from acting inhumane and ensuring that we do not give in to the areas within ourselves where animal behaviors reside. It is worth knowing that nature and nurture are strongly intertwined, as one without the other is just not practical. One simple example: a woman suffers from malnutrition, or she or her partner, or both, have a smoking habit or are addicted to drugs or alcohol. Perhaps these individuals are entangled in web of uncertainty and find themselves in a helpless and hopeless situation, full of stress and anxiety. Then, accidently or by choice, they learn they are having a baby. The medical community has proven that the pregnancy is less likely to be a healthy one, and the baby born less likely to be salubrious and wholesome. Unless the entire set of negative criteria are reversed and replaced with proper nurturing and a life of benevolence, decent enough to bring about the right results for reproduction and pregnancy, the child already starts out with unfavorable odds.

Thomas Jefferson, in *Letters of Thomas Jefferson*, said, "Nobody wishes more than I do to see such proofs as you exhibit, that nature has given to our black brethren, talents equal to those of the other colors of men, and that the appearance of a want of them is owing merely to the degraded condition of their existence, both in Africa & America." I frankly do not really decipher why so much commotion exists about "genes," since our innate nature is hugely influenced by where and how we live our lives. Do geopolitical and economic situations not affect our lives? Does it not depend on our lifestyles, which need to be resourceful and lived within a healthy environment free of pressure and tension? The food we consume, the water we drink, the air we breathe, and how much fun and happiness we get out of life, affect us. We are harmed not by the almighty God; but by our own kind which deliver miseries to billions, negatively affecting their lives. In this, we should by the reason of sanity expect unhealthy genes to be dominant due to so many living in horrifying conditions. If not, we must live in a world of fiction and hallucination and not a real one.

The reality is, we are case-sensitive. Do we respond to stress? Yes. Do we respond to the fact that we are not immune to fear? Yes. Do we respond to malnutrition? Yes. Do we respond to lack of sleep and inadequate rest? Yes. Do we respond to chemically produced food and GMOS? Yes. Do we respond to the polluted air we breathe? Yes. Do we negatively respond to a drug-infested environment, smoking, alcoholism, unhygienic conditions? Yes. Family violence, poverty, anxiety, loneliness and lack of love and in not having somewhere to belong? Yes. All this, and a host of other manufactured and troubling issues.

The truth is that we are affected by both the good and bad situations, which in return can impact us either positively or negatively. If we are adversely impacted, then it aborts our chances of producing healthy and potent genes to pass along to a vibrant fetus, and eventually to a healthy child. If we believe this not to be the case, then we are ignoring many scientific, medical, and counseling professionals who advise against a lifestyle filled with violence and stress. They also recommend not using drugs or alcohol, avoiding tobacco smoke, and encourage a loving and caring environment, especially if couples are planning a pregnancy. We need to honestly ask ourselves: if this is not the case, why then, are there so many physical and mental illnesses? Why are there so many complicated pregnancies, so many birth defects, and so many unhealthy babies? The fact is, we are not cursed by God or Satan or nature and/or by any other manufactured reason. We are being lied to and structurally exploited; we are not appropriately nurtured and we are stranded from the truth.

Many adamantly believe their genes are responsible for some of their misfortunes and health-related issues, their intelligence, emotions, their looks and other physical features—this could relatively be the case. But it is also true that shortcomings and weaknesses in the human animal could be positively altered if we are able to systemically and professionally attend to people's dire situations. It always pays to do good deeds, perhaps not immediately, but certainly in the long run. It is just how nature works, gradually but surely. This is the era of consciousness, where people are thorough and inquisitive on vital issues and how decisions that impact their lives are made. Where these issues are misleading and attempts to make such decisive matters convoluted are keenly questioned, many fabricated issues are exposed. James Boswell (1740-1795) states, "Wickedness is always easier than virtue, for it takes the shortcut to everything." And Plutarch, the Greek philosopher, said: "Character is simply habit long continued." And I say: "let's make decent environments to give birth to excellence." Ralph Waldo Emerson wrote that, "...man is a bundle of relations, a knot of roots whose flower and fruitage is the world..." Do not fall for a second into believing this is how God made you, and that your genetic shortcomings can't be overcome. You must defend yourself against such fabricated lies and unrealities; one can always change for the better.

Bruce Lipton, a professor of cell biology says, "It is not about genetic determinism which many believe that genes control life, traits, behaviors, your physical characteristics, etc. It is about the environment which profoundly effects the very essence of our being." Mr. Lipton experimented with this by placing the same cell with identical genes into different environments. He found out the environment acts like a cultural medium; different results were manifested under different conditions. He attests to the fact that a suitable environment providing good water, air, and food created healthy, vibrant cells. When the conditions were reversed, no good cells were ever produced. Mr. Lipton also points out that many scientists have addressed epigenetic control (epi meaning "above"). This new science now shows that we are not the victims of our hereditary status, and that we are the ones who control our genes. Research reveals that how one responds to one's environment is how one is able to change his or her fate. It is seen as an anomaly and a big mistake to marginalize and not see the truth in how very important the impact of the environment on human cells and the genome is. Further, if we exhaust all of our God-given talents, nothing can stop us in acquiring miracles, and in flourishing and conquering the impossible. This should help us to answer the huge question of "why are we here?"

Yes, we must help humanity defend itself against ignorance and its ramifications. We must put our minds to work, and ask big questions; even if it looks like we are dreaming, there is no shame in that. The proclivity of our intelligence will eventually reach its proper state of mind and rightly so, to someday proudly live the impossible. I utter this, since our brains are extremely malleable and have infinite potential to be rewired again and again to where the magic and marvels of life await us. We can gradually encourage our minds to reach their maximum potentials, molding them skillfully where they can advance to the next plateau—resulting in peak performance again and again.

Blind people rewire their brains; the visual cortex becomes an accessory, allowing other senses to becoming more powerful, such as significant development of their sense of hearing and the ability to learn to navigate through what is called "echolocation." When we are learning new skills through training and adapting to thought-provoking ideas, new neurons are created in our brain. Our brains are congenial to specific traits and professions which we undertake and follow. One can practically mold and modify one's own brain, since brain plasticity makes it possible to enter into new domains, strengthening one's rationality and discernment. We will one day become acquainted with and able to manage other planets, and perhaps discover the extraterrestrial world. Humans should be able to reach the stars and make advances in other galaxies, overcoming what seems practically impossible.

We need to connect to the natural forces of the universe, and learn how best to make them applicable in advancing our lives. If we can accomplish this, then we will shall ride on waves of energy so potent that nothing will stop us in accomplishing the impossible. And we must insist on reaching the reality of a greater mind, where we never again have to face dilemmas that lure us into helplessness and discouragement. Interacting with our surroundings and learning more about them as we experience new things is how we develop our brains to go to the next level. There are a host of stages that take place when we acquire new knowledge.

The ingenuity behind most talented endeavors is not because of one having a sixth sense, as some irrationally claim. It is because one's five senses are so utterly focused and immersed in one's thoughts that it seems to the undertaker that no time, space, or any other matter actually exists, except that which has colossally mesmerized him. He is so immersed in his thought process, as if hypnotized into a realm other than ours. It may appear as though he has arrived into the zone, into the quantum field, obsessed with the moment and so insightful as to be able to answer any abstract thought clearly and meaningfully as he explains his powerful discoveries. In conclusion, our genes can have an enormous effect on our behaviors, but then our environment collaborates to mold our personalities and attributes. The internal and the external worlds both play a huge role into who we really are.

Essay 9

I, and then I, Again and Again I, to the Day I Die

I am, as you are: biological, biochemical, bio hormonal, biophysical, biomechanical, bio-neurological, psychological, and bio-conscious. We are social, moral, spiritual, and also temporal and emotional. We are as well a part of eternity. Let's not forget being methodological, as we are also scientific and mystical. But who is this "I." Am I my senses, and am I what I think and perceive? There are those who believe our senses do have their limits, and that what is perceived by our human senses could be wrong. What we perceive as fact may not be true and is dismissed as only imagination; in other words what we see is not the *only* truth. Am I my physical body, made of bones, joints, muscles, ligaments, vital organs, blood, cells, arteries, veins, fat, and nerves? The physical body is in need of constant attention, and who is the "I" who should pay attention to this ceaselessly changing body until the day it dies—does this "I" really exist? There are those who say it does not; this has created controversial views between philosophers and scholarly-minded scientists over the course of our human history.

Who is this silent conductor, the driving force behind my thoughts— am I really in control of my mind? And the choices I make, the supposedly autonomous decisions that I render? These decisions are rewarded when good and punished if otherwise; sometimes making the wrong decision can even make or break me. Are we, the free-willed and able-bodied, to be predestined, and enslaved by our fate? Could it be that no matter what I choose to be, either delinquent in action and behavior or diligent and disciplined, my destiny is mapped and planned? No matter the outcome, perhaps I will be confined by my fate in a designated square, predestined and the victim of an already orchestrated verdict. Or maybe I was previously nominated to win the winning lottery ticket of life, determined to live a life of plenty. Who is this character that sometimes gets tired of living, so pressured and furiously upset that he decides to terminate it all, so that he does not witness and feel so much anguish and suffering for the human race?

Who is this "I" that is in pain when others are hurting, who adamantly seeks answers and perseveres in finding a solution? Who is the invisible force that tirelessly nags and questions, "What, if any, constructive actions did you take to help others in need?" What about when I am in love— elated, so happy with life— and then no matter who else is in pain, I act carefree, like a wild horse, as if others do not exist? Who is this "I" in my dreams, in my thoughts, that I worry about— even after I supposedly expire? It seems when we look to observe the self, we only see awareness, which cannot be located in our physical body or neural network. If there is a spirit or a soul, where is it? Who is responsible for all that we do?

It is not about Darwinism; it is about conscious awareness. It is about the cosmic energy that is the impetus and the driving force behind all our activities; it is about the intelligence behind a single cell multiplying into one hundred cells and exponentially growing to billions and trillions of cells. A mind so vast should lead us to believe that we do not live in space and time, but that time and space lives in our mind. Many physicists and others in related scientific fields have shed light on some of the uncertainties of the unseen world, where beyond molecules and subatomic particles is *nothing*, which makes us believe we came from nothing—but a nothing that is apparently beyond our comprehension of what is known as the void or empty space, as it is then somehow impregnated with everything.

What is clear is that the answer does not lie in Darwinism, which was nothing but a hoax by the empire of wealth and power, the super-rich and the ruling class to create a deliberate genetic farce to control and exploit the so-called inferior race. According to Darwin's theory, they are not fit enough to manage their lives, because they are closer to apes than human beings. Darwin, in *The Origin of Species* (1859) explains, "All organic beings that have lived on Earth could be descended from some primordial form." Perhaps we should further dig into "natural selection" to find answers to our ambiguous and puzzling questions on the origin of life.

European Neanderthals had a brain closest to that of modern man; other ancient humans found in Africa and Asia were subspecies that had to be ruled by the superior race. Perhaps in the near future, any remaining race-related problems will be eradicated since multiculturalism and an environment of multi-ethnicity is gravitating toward miscegenation. Eventually, race uniformity will likely overcome race problems in their entirety. Other doctrines that expect the individual to be ethically paramount are geared to the concept that all rights and rewards, values, interests, duties and tasks should originate in the individual. This theory stresses political and economic separation and independence from pluralism, which is pragmatic when one pursues such theory. As a matter of fact, the exact opposite has been scientifically proven—that being cooperative is the most productive and fruitful for everyone.

Yes, people should be able to follow their wildest dreams and to do all that is in their power to reach their full potential. But it should also be realized that if a good life for everyone is not collectively bargained for, we will all be heading for a dead end, eventually finding ourselves bogged down in the trenches of life. Frederic Bastiat said, "When plunder becomes a way of life for a group of men living together in society, they create for themselves in the course of time a legal system that authorizes it and a moral code that glorifies it." Jesus of Nazareth said, "It is easier for a camel to pass through the eye of a needle than for a rich man to enter the kingdom of God." So it is not about any earthy theory or so-called scientific endeavor when others are in search of the origin of life; many of the theories that win Nobel prizes in one way or another link the origin of life to normalizing, naturalizing and legitimizing the exploitation of the commonwealth and natural resources, including human-beings.

The truth is, with respect to the search for an answer to the origin of life, most prominent scientists are lost and do not have a clue where consciousness comes from, where is it located, and how life started. This encourages humanity to look upon the intervention of a divine hand as responsible for the origin of life, something from the cosmic and heavenly domain, not found in earthy theories and doctrine. The fact is that consciousness not only exits in humans, but in every animated being, including animals, plants, and other taxa. However, this awareness is represented in different shapes and forms within a variety of categorical species, since their anatomical structures and nervous systems are built much different than those of human beings, and in some ways function at an even higher level than those of humans.

There are millions of instances demonstrating that animals become aware of the paranormal, and sense disasters that are about to happen. The uncanny but true stories that credit dogs, cats, and other beasts with having a sixth sense and a strong premonition to detect trouble way ahead of humans has helped them to survive. How can an eagle detect a fish under the water miles away and hunt it with extreme accuracy? How about bats that maneuver in the dark with astonishing clarity, or roosters that crow at the exact time every dawn, like a very expensive Swiss watch? Could it be that we are so limited in our perception of reality and what is actually happening without even knowing it? Should we not notice the unconditional love that dogs show to their owners, and how they recognize and protect them when their sharp senses of smell and sound detect happenings much more quickly than their humans?

It actually gets more complicated when psychologists and psychotherapists like Sigmund Freud, the father of modern psychology, elaborate on how the human brain functions. The triple mentality of "id, ego, and super ego," is an interesting theory that has dominated the world of psychology for more than a century, based on Freud's testimony and structural models of the psyche. Each of these behave in a specific way and with exclusive apparatus, making one wonder in which state we really reside. Perhaps we can reside in all three at the same time? To make a long story short, the id is tied to our animal instincts and our lower self, in search of immediate gratification and indulging in pleasure related tasks, looking for the "good life" and other enjoyments. The super ego often acts in opposition to the id; it behaves as a father figure, and ties directly to morality and a mentality of good conduct. Super ego mediates when our animal instincts activate and are bound to put us in trouble. It can be identified as a spiritual teacher which manifests our higher self. Then there is ego, the reality-oriented apparatus. Ego mediates between the id and reality, helping perhaps to avoid grief and destruction, and trying to harness our sometimes irrational thoughts. With that said, who are really the movers and the shakers behind these complex urges and desires, hopes and emotions, and sometimes radical feelings? Who is really there?

Let's consider these scientific findings not as hypothesis but as theories, which should make us question where this enigmatic and invisible force that causes such exhilarating behaviors (sometimes beyond imagination or belief) comes from, Could it be the same energy that applies to electromagnetic forces, gravity, and big and small atomic energies? Could it be the same energy that is in accord with quantum mechanics and string theory, which predict eleven parallel universes and other unheard of ideas? If it ever materialized, such energy would be nothing short of a miracle.

As the physicists now hypothesize a world made up of more than three dimensions—and perhaps eleven dimensions, which mathematically fits their findings—if substantiated, this must be the heaven promised. Humans should be honored and truly addressed as the image of God himself on planet Earth. And then perhaps we will quit this narcissism and become more in tune with our higher selves and our true human nature. We could move far, far away from inhumane actions, and no longer give meaning to the reality of hell; we could simply "live and let live."

We have reached a progressive state in our evolutionary awareness that should halt us from seeing the world in only physical and material terms. There are those "doctoring" that suggest that the whole of human progress and the physical world is the embodiment of a testosterone-driven mechanism, which is the major reason for our progress and human civility. Such absurd messages applied to an already ill human body and sick mind will further result in a chaotic life. We are experiencing it now, as we slaughter each other over territories, possessions, and individual gratuity, evil desires with no propriety or sincere claims to human decency.

Some of us do not see this energy-driven cosmos and the heaven above, and choose to become blind as bats, not realizing that it is the unseen world that rules the physical world. It becomes hard for our human software and compassionate nature to be truly applied when we act like robots, programmed to be habitual and routine, in a trance of addiction to the material world and forced to bear its ugly consequences. Either way, Frederick Douglass' expression, "Knowledge makes a man unfit to be a slave" can only become reality when one realizes the potential one has to reach the stars, to know that ninety-nine percent of our troubles are truly man made. The only reason we do not realize this potential is ignorance. Unless we become enlightened and impressively educated, and acquire wisdom and compassion, we will always be treated as part of the herd. Karl Marx, God bless his soul, explains that as workers, we are all alienated from (1) the product of our labor (2) the labor process (3) our fellow human beings (society), and (4) our own human nature or species-being. This in turn has affected society and caused us all severe ill will, with bloodied repercussions in our private and public lives. Humanity must stop discriminating against each other and must stop destroying its habitat. We need to discard and stop empowering doctrines and theories that are deliberately prejudiced against mankind.

Natural selection favors the survival of some of variations over others and made Darwin believe that only the strong are to survive; he therefore titled his findings as "The Survival of the Fittest." But it is collectivism and teamwork that boils from the essence of nature, since it favors God and the essence of who we are. Look, here is the deal: if people are not able to afford the most basic necessities of life such as food, water, clean air, housing, a good education, and efficient medical facilities, they just won't be happy. Since we are all interconnected with each other and nature, this is going to affect us all sooner or later in the most horrible of ways.

These unsatisfactory conditions should not be taken lightly because people have the potential to erupt like volcanos as history has confirmed many times. But if and when you cut the economical gaps and allocate the resources in a fair and moderate manner, by creating jobs with financial and social safety nets and coverage for all, it will be true human rights in the making. This most definitely brings about a win-win situation for everyone, instead of prosperity for a few and misery for the majority of people. Only then would the calamities of greed, selfishness, and egocentrism not behold us all. We must realize that perhaps the survival of the fittest is possible in the animal kingdom; but in humans it is almost impossible, since we are all intertwined. What one does will affect others in one way or another, and it is certainly the wrong road to travel.

Life is a caravan that carries a variety of colorful products and diversified commodities, but it should move in concert and together, since no child of God should be left behind. It is time to promote universal values, and think in terms of "humanity;" any other priorities should be directed towards that objective, and should not become delinquent from this very vital task. This should remind us of the 13th century Persian poet "Sa'adi Shirazi." who, of humanity, wrote:

> Human beings are members of a whole,
> In creation of one essence and soul.
> If one member is afflicted with pain,
> Other members uneasy will remain.
> If you've no sympathy for human pain,
> The name of human you cannot retain.

Essay 10
A Few Perils of Our Time

It is nice to feel proud to live in places and environments that promote lawful behaviors and protect social civility in the way we deal with our lives. Let's consider only one concerning issue out of millions, and test it to see how true this claim of civility really is. Furthermore, should it even be lawful? Let's not go too far; let's just look at the food we eat and the consequences that we have to bear. Is it civilized to use psychological techniques uniquely devised with gimmicks to get people to consume food that we know is going to make them sick? Is it right to still insist on bringing it to the marketplace and to sell it, not informing the consumers of the potential dire effects, all in the name of business, profit, and free enterprise? David Brownstein, M.D., says, "Genetically modified (GM) foods may look and feel the same as conventional foods, but they are drastically (and possibly harmfully) different. These types of foods have been altered by taking the genetic material (DNA) from one species and transferring it into another in order to obtain a desired trait. The FDA does not require any safety testing or any labeling of GM foods, and introducing new genes into a fruit or vegetable may very well be creating unknown results such as new toxins, new bacteria, new allergens, and new diseases."

Look, it is not like one has to be a rocket scientist to notice the host of killer diseases that have arisen from these chemically saturated and genetically modified foods. They have most definitely affected our natural hormonal balances, and are causing so many horrible health issues that even the most advanced medical providers are sometimes unable to treat them. I suspect that genetically altered foods play a role in the development of cardiovascular disease and heart problems, strokes, multiple cancer diagnoses, immunodeficiency disorders, hormonal imbalance, multiple sclerosis, Alzheimer's disease and dementia, Parkinson's disease, lupus, liver and kidney disease, chronic fatigue syndrome, joint problems, birth defects and infertility, arthritis, diabetes, degenerative nerve diseases, depression, multiple personality disorder, bipolar disorder, thyroid disease, gum and tooth problems, horrifying rashes, amnesia, schizophrenia, autism, mad cow disease, salmonella, high blood pressure, high cholesterol, obesity, impotency, asthma, allergies, degenerative diseases, Ebola, and respiratory problems. All of these and hundreds more killer diseases are induced because of toxic chemical exposure to these food products and artificial ingredients such as trans fats, high fructose syrup, artificial sweeteners, sodium sulfite, sodium nitrite, sulfur dioxide, potassium bromate, monosodium glutamate, citric acid (used for flavoring), and BHA/BHT (added to keep fat from going rancid). During processing, poisonous additives, bleach, MSG, preservatives, artificial colors, and even antibiotics are added. At the same time, natural ingredients are extracted from these foods.

As a result of this, millions of people and counting die every year. Jean-Jacques Rousseau stated, "God (Nature, in my view) makes all things good; man meddles with them and they become evil. He fores one soil to yield the products of another, one tree to bear another's fruit. He confuses and confounds time, place, and natural conditions. He mutilates his dog, his horse, and his slave. He destroys and defaces all things; he loves all that is deformed and monstrous; he will have nothing as nature made it, not even himself, who must learn his paces like a saddle-horse, and be shaped to his master's taste like the trees in his garden."

There is not a single soul in our civilized society who can effectively stop this madness; we must become collectively enlightened and resist the temptation and deliberate attempt to fool us into buying and consuming their harmful products. As they enjoy their lives in island paradises eating wholesome foods bought with our hard earned money, we buy intoxicated foods, and they hypnotically watch us die like programmed robots. So what should be the proper response? It would perhaps be next to none, if we are not adamantly educating people to eat organically-grown nutritious foods with healthy ingredients like natural vitamins and minerals. "Biotechnology and GM crops are taking us down a dangerous road, creating the classic conditions for hunger, poverty and even famine. Ownership and control concentrated in too few hands and a food supply based on too few varieties of crops planted widely are the worst option for food security." (Christian Aid report, "Biotechnology and GMOs.) Tom Wiley, a North Dakota farmer, says, "Farmers are being sued for having GMOs on their property that they did not buy, do not want, will not use, and cannot sell." It is funny, then, perhaps hilarious; we are never short on lecturing people to eat wholesome foods with plenty of nutrients, made from organic ingredients, to achieve an active and healthy lifestyle. We don't think about the masses of people that cannot even afford high-calorie salty, fatty, sugary processed foods filled with chemicals. Most of them know that what they are consuming is for sure going to either make them sick, or act as a catalyst toward an early death, killing them by adding obesity to high blood pressure with a whole host of other related problems—in some cases impossible to cure. Many people have near-death experiences due to hunger and malnutrition, again a byproduct of our supposedly fair and economical way of life. We need to ask why the more technological and industrialized we become, the further we stray from wisdom, and the more we give in to turpitude. If not greed or in the name of doing mischievous business, then, what is it? I did not know it was ok to harm others, sentencing so many who are caught in a wretched financial dilemma to their early death. They are damned if they do, and damned if they don't, because billions who live below the poverty line cannot in any way afford organic and wholesome food. They have no choice but to eat what is less expensive, which is very harmful, since these foods are saturated with chemicals and killing agents.

There are so many who are anxious to know where their next meal will come from. Not having enough to survive causes millions of families so much stress; it is beyond tragic. Is there a day that goes by that some members of such a poverty afflicted household do not think of suicide? They suffer as they deal with hardship, earning less than two dollars a day and enduring mental anguish, even seeing their loved ones waste away and perish in front of their eyes because of poverty. Wisdom dictates that when the wealth of eighty-five individuals is equal to the wealth of half of the world's population, what else should anyone expect other than misery for the rest of the world? Then we witness the media, the government, and other business entities preach to these people: "Oh, become educated, become enlightened. Eat organic and powerful foods with vitamins, minerals, and low calories. Take a trip once in a while, have regular check-ups, enjoy time with family." I wonder how enjoyable it will be to live within a family that does not have shelter, must live on one meal a day, is not able to afford education or heath care, and has nothing nice to wear. This is sometimes despite the fact that they work very hard to make a decent living, but cannot. Some choose not to even notice people's financial depravity, miseries, and what they actually have to go through to afford even this toxic food. It is nothing but a farce to claim to profess care and concern for humankind. Former Democratic representative Dennis Kucinich said, "The FDA has received over 1,000,000 comments from citizens demanding labeling of GMOs, 90% of American agree. So, why no labeling? I'll give you one reason: the influence and corruption of the political process by Monsanto."

It is time to wake up and smell the coffee. There are millions of people that can perhaps only *smell* good food as they are passing by a high class restaurant in a rich neighborhood. That is, of course, if they are not apprehended and arrested for trespassing. What I am saying is this: let's stop insulting people's intelligence. Stop making those in poverty the subject of unending jokes and humorous views. It is time to realistically address our genuine social and economic predicaments and difficulties, with honest and decent intention. We must let people live a life that is meant to be happy and free from financial stress, not one filled with manufactured maneuvers and deliberate plans to fool them. The current status quo, "the rich getting richer and the poor becoming poorer," can no longer persist; the poor are not even able afford the bare minimum, many become paupers and homeless. Acting negligent and careless toward these problems facing humanity has led to many adverse effects in our lives; we are already spending billions of dollars trying to fix the tsunami of evil outcomes pushing the limits of humanity, while more are still to come.

The destruction of billions of lives has become an epidemic. Perhaps the ongoing epidemic serves some people and entities well, such as those who want to preserve their positions of wealth and power by depopulating the world. If this not the case, what else could be the motive behind this madness? If we convince ourselves that it is "just doing business," then the question becomes, "should we be in the business of destroying people's health when premature death and sickness is the end result?" Adam Leith Gollner says, "If manufacturers are so sure there is nothing wrong with genetically modified foods, pesticides and cloned meats, they should have no problems labeling them as such. 'After all, cancer will kill one in every two men and one in every three women now alive,' reports Samuel Epstein, chairman of the Cancer Prevention Coalition. Like our ancestors, we act in ways that will bemuse future societies. The military-industrial complex lubricates the mass-agriculture system with fossil fuels. Tons of heavy metals and other hazardous, even radioactive, waste is sprayed on American agricultural soil." The bottom line is that genetically modified foods are quickly and surreptitiously being imposed upon the world food market with seemingly no regard for studies that indicate that they are extremely harmful. Are we in need of a renaissance?

Our perception of so-called reality needs to be changed, because the reality we conceptualize is very much based on inhumane standards and unethical attitudes; for example: if one is killed, there is bound to be punishment, but when millions are slaughtered—genocide—we simply see it as how history is played out. There is something very wrong in our judgment of what is wrong and what is right. Sadly, we are conditioned to set our priorities based on narrow-mindedness, not understanding the truth behind cultural and racial differences, nationalism, religious beliefs, economic status and class differentiations, gender bias, and our own arrogance and self-interest in accumulating wealth and power at any cost. Such priorities are not based on human dignity and the preservation of life and justice, or in the name of peace, morality, and the common good. The entire population of planet Earth is a force to be reckoned with and individuals should not be seen as lacking in mental acuity and physical prowess just because they are poor. They should not be considered handicapped in aptitude or in the spiritual arena, such that even God has cursed them, and for a no-good reason, too.

I say, then: are we not due for another renaissance, leading to a whole revival and Cultural Revolution that changes everything? One that can prevail in a peaceful manner and without bloodshed? Or am I dreaming when I wish for such a peaceful endeavor? Because when we look at the course of human history in a realistic way, we notice almost all drastically altered societies and nations that have uprooted their archaic systems to bring about social justice have given birth to violence. This is a sacrifice beyond imagination in terms of lives, property, and belongings vital to their very survival. Pope John Paul II said, "Social justice cannot be attained by violence. Violence kills what it intends to create." Text within the Dhammapada, the sacred scriptures of Theravada Buddhism, states, "All men fear pain and death, all men love life. Remembering that he is one of them, let a man neither strike nor kill." But then come to think of it, truly constructive change occurs gradually and through the evolutionary process; it happens quiescently, causing no trouble, and within appropriate time parameters.

Could it possibly be true that our minds, our consciousness, and our abilities to reason and make good decisions have halted, and stopped growing? Are we not hallucinating, thinking all of our troubles should perhaps disappear through revolution, war machines and violence? No viable and promising change can take place without collective wisdom and the positive power of thinking to boost our knowledge and information. Science tells us for a fact that our ancient predecessors, perhaps along the scale of millions of years ago, had to gradually expand their prefrontal cortex into a thinking machine, evolving to the progressive state of mind necessary for today's modern age. It just puzzles me: I ask myself over and over if we have perhaps reached our brain's biological and evolutionary limit. If this is the case, then future outcomes shall be disappointing as there is no hope left for our brain to further extend its biological and mental processes. If this is not the case and there is still room for our brain to grow and render even more progressive faculty, why then, do we need to resolve our differences by hostile means and violence? Why do so many innocent lives need to be taken, and why should so much pain and suffering occur, literally every day? So much is nonchalantly ignored that we feel our beastly side is rather in charge of our welfare and destiny.

Have we not yet reached a point in our evolutionary track to detect a decisive maturity of mind and character? Is it not true that our wisdom and thoughts should be more advanced and civilized than our ancestors? Evolution should mean moving from simplicity to higher stages of maturity and completeness. Why is it so difficult to let go of our pride and many other social, cultural, political and economic ills that are unnecessary and problematic? They are endangering our lives and effecting our very livelihood.

If we honestly believe in the evolution of mind and decent behavior, does it not make sense to take preventive measures to correct these maladies and disorderly conduct in our lives? Helen Keller said, "Until the great mass of people shall be filled with the sense of responsibility for each other's welfare, social justice cannot be attained." In other words, no social revolution will be fruitful until the revolution of mind, consciousness, and social responsibility prevails. We need to awaken to the host of lies deliberately implanted within our thought processes and embedded in the way we live. It should not be difficult to detect lies and apocalyptic rhetoric in the theory that our natural resources are growing exponentially and our human population is growing numerically, therefore we can afford an overpopulated world. This cannot be any further from the truth.

Do we not realize that something must be done to control the population growth, and that we need to reconsider our criteria for overpopulation? Why do we not learn from the lessons history teaches us? When people go hungry, there is be war and revolution with catastrophic measures. Tell me if this overconsumption and excessive waste by the few, leading to and hunger and malnutrition, sometimes epidemic disease for the millions, if not billions of poor is a virtue and not a vice. So many do not have the very basic necessities of life: clean drinking water, a roof overhead, education, basic sanitation, medical and health coverage, decent jobs, and are forced to migrate like wild animals and flocks of birds to survive.

The system should be the proponent of the right to life, individual freedom, human rights, democracy, property rights, and the pursuit of happiness and liberty for all while respecting others' sovereignty; many nations with progressive constitutions say so. But honestly, how can anyone have the right to life without health coverage and assistance with the cost of needed medicines? Are we not aware that millions, if not billions, are deprived of their right to live healthy lives? These individuals are unable to manage a decent living and die from illness because they are unable to afford medical attention related to famine, hunger, basic sanitation, contaminated water and polluted air, contagious diseases, drought, tsunami, climate change and global warming, apartheid rulings, wars of aggression, forced migration, and discrimination. I wonder how life and the pursuit of happiness is ever possible for the many without faces and voices.

How can anyone turn a blind eye to the very important fact that people must have decent vocations to be able to make it, as they need to be productive in this complex monetary and fiscal system? Is it not true that when people are pushed to their limit and held against the wall, they will become unruly and violent as their survival mode kicks in, regardless of how much power is available to quell their uprising? I think the responsible parties should respect and pay attention to their prefrontal cortex, their so-called "thinking brain," and do something constructive to resolve these, and hundreds of other issues in urgent need of repair. They need to stop spending billions funding crooks and political parties that are up to no good for humanity. They need to stop the looting and pillaging of the nation by Wall Street and similar entities in other parts of the world that are globally tied. Unless we develop a yardstick to measure our moral and ethical conduct, including how to behave in comparison to absolute goodness, we will sink further into this horrible quicksand.

It is fair to mention that a society can survive many dangerous and unexpected perils unless its judiciary system becomes unreliable. Societies should make sure that the authorities in charge enforce and uphold the law, and are impervious to the temptation of any wrongdoing. It is crucial that legislatures, judges, juries and prosecutors keep their political views and beliefs completely autonomous and absolutely detached from influencing their verdict or any decisions relying on their judgment in the court of law. It must be understood by the officers of the law and police authorities that the time has come where they will be held accountable if they stray from exactly what the law dictates. Authorities need to pay attention to avoid police brutality; unarmed people are being shot, sometimes in the back, prior to being proven guilty in a court of law.

If the legislative, judicial, and executive branches of law, either at the state or federal level, are not prudent or ultimately become dysfunctional, then there is truly no hope for the nation to maintain peace and societal tranquility. Unfortunately justice is not always a priority. Sometimes, despite compelling evidence, a person with no fortune or fame is seen as one who is "guilty as charged until proven innocent." Bear in mind when one is not able to hire good legal help, it is next to impossible to find freedom again. There is a saying, "if you are rich and guilty, you are treated better than if you are poor and innocent." Money talks, and the one who spends the most talks the loudest. Charles de Montesquieu proclaims, "There is no crueler tyranny than that which is perpetuated under the shield of law and in the name of justice," and John Witherspoon adds, "The people in general ought to have regard to the moral character of those whom they invest with authority either in the legislative, executive, or judicial branches." despite our modern advancements in all sorts of technologies, and our claims of civility in mind and manner, we are vacillating in our faith and belief in the absolute almighty God, and are acting complacent toward the urgent changes that must take place. Potentially colossal hazards are facing us all. It is also true that no matter what we say or utter in theory, unless it is coupled with decent and righteous deeds, it is of no use and should otherwise only be regarded as empty rhetoric. And I believe it is overwhelmingly true that unless any judiciary system insists on the presumption of innocence until proven guilty beyond the shadow of a doubt, no justice is ever served.

It is quite odd knowing that despite the advanced forensic science available to the courts, unparalleled expertise, creativity and skill in interrogation, and readily available sophisticated psychological and psychiatric techniques, so many innocent victims are still sent to the electric chair, are awaiting execution, or sentenced to life in prison. After the damage is done, the law authorities realize their grave mistakes and yet those who are responsible for such tragic malefactions enjoy impunity. Can we not mandate laws to hold responsible parties accountable for their folly and utterly negligent behaviors and misconduct? It could save innocent lives when suspects are entangled in a web of uncertainty, caught in a state of legal limbo filled with red tape and bureaucracy, until the smoke clears. We must comprehend exactly what transpired before sending innocent people to their death chambers. I am certain the odds will not be against those blessed with enough money to afford a competent and well-known attorney who literally protects them every step of the way. In contrast, the poor must endure treacherous and sometimes deliberate evil lurking in the dark, filled with racial bias and prejudicial profiling, and ill judgment already made against them before being proven guilty. The poor are unfairly victimized, and many are not competent and professional enough to manage the intricacy of the criminal proceedings. The vitality of judiciary decision-making must be scrutinized, since human life and one's very freedom is at stake.

It is sad to see that the ultra-rich and the privileged few are treated above the law, and are basically immune to legal punishment since they are automatically leveraged to buy the best legal help available. The poor cannot afford to hire legal help, which should tell us much about the travesty of the law and looming threat. This situation is not going to change unless we are awakened to the need for education and enlightenment in this area, exercising mindfulness and providing dynamic training on complicated social issues and criminal justice. We cannot be dumbfounded in the process, otherwise we become the victims of our emotions and feelings; these can play catalyst to the bewilderment and ultimately put us in the wrong side of justice. Our feelings and emotions are a double edged sword, fueled by compassion, kindness, integrity and sacrifice on one side; and yet fueled with hatred and resentment on the other side. It is a very fine line to either walk and act as our higher self, or otherwise behave from our lower beastly side, which can lead to horrific deeds of genocide, trampling justice and humiliating decency.

Charlatans and demagogues know how to take advantage of people through sentiment and feelings, they purposely cause people's emotions to go every which way, like a roller coaster. Hitler was a good example of wickedness and demagoguery, piercing through people's emotions and souls, causing so much pain and suffering as millions of Jews were slaughtered. Let's not forget the genocide in Bosnia where millions of Muslims were killed, Mussolini's rhetoric that destroyed millions of innocent lives, or Franco of Spain—all in the name of nationalism, patriotism, race, ethnicity, and religion. Another type of terrorism is led by spirited cult leaders that impersonate good and faithful religious pedagogues by invading people's spirits and emotions in the name of some type of God—at the same time deploying hatred and inhumane activities for their self-interest, causing the death and destruction of many. We must learn not to become victims of any sort of molding or conditioning, since these inhumane approaches can demoralize people and make them act devilish. We are all from the same human family and original race; no one is made of a lesser God. We should neither act naïve and easily become fooled, nor let anyone misrepresent who we really are as good human beings. We ought to be cultured and enlightened, as true human beings should, so that some evil–minded, self-interested beast cannot make us vulnerable enough to perform misdeeds. Such misdeeds could potentially put our lives on the line, leaving our consciences, thoughts, emotions, and our very lives at their mercy.

These leaders have learned how to quarantine people, conditioning them with their huge influence and might. They have access to all the power and the ingredients necessary to invade the population subtlety, just like a microorganism would invade healthy bodies. It time to wake up and smell the coffee, to stand our ground—because it is the age of consciousness and the revolution of the minds! It is not the era to manufacture lies, fabrications, and demagogueries anymore; the leaders are acting as incendiaries, urging us to fall prey to their inflammatory and rabble rousing means.

No matter what our real source of misfortune may be, what is necessary to understand is that human beings are wired to goodness and caring, compassion, conscientiousness and kindness? We all belong to one source; we are an undeniable part of the almighty God and cosmic consciousness. If we do not defy the atrocious and notorious acts and become vigilant in detecting the false promises designed to enslave us, we show nothing short of the characteristics of a boor. False promises can play on us either through our emotions or by economic means, which can put the masses at the mercy of moguls, where our sovereignty becomes questionable and we are not respected as human beings, but seen as labor-producing machines. These ugly varieties of misconduct and the looting of justice should make a human revival in consciousness a must; we are in urgent need of a worldly renaissance.

We know that between the advertising industry, superbly advanced technology now available to media, and the ongoing propaganda machine, people can be conditioned in a heartbeat. Why not deliberately make it your business to make a serious attempt to motivate people and to make enough resources available for them to become truly knowledgeable in understanding their rights and how to defend them? If this happens, they will not be so exploited by almost everything that is supposed to shield them and provide immunity; for example: cultural, political, legal, social and financial perils are failing them in almost everything they are trying to positively accomplish. Abigail Adams says, "Learning is not attained by chance, it must be sought for with ardor and diligence." It would truly be a deed of humanitarian patronage, appreciated like never before, and poised to remind the world of the kind and aspiring work that can be done on behalf of humanity. Such a deed would never be forgotten.

Essay 11
Does the Soul Exist?

Recent scientific theory speaks to life's spiritual parameters; this refers to the reality of the soul, among many other affiliated and vital issues in our lives. Religions relentlessly remind us about its existence. How do we know if the soul really exists? A series of new scientific experiments shed light on this primordial spiritual question. The question of the soul is raised with the idea of a future life and our beliefs about the next realm of existence. It is an animated yet subtle issue which permeates our thoughts, where it cannot be reflected upon through scientific analysis. This characteristic has since has created skeptics who misunderstand such potent energy. At the same time, the enlightened are relentlessly curious, wanting to know about its manifestation independent from our physical body.

The human soul, like the mind, is not visible, however it is as important and exceedingly even more likely to evoke our curiosity. Our mind, although not perceived through tactile senses, plays a very significant role in our mental and cognitive activities—only unlike the soul, its effects are known and the evidence is physically substantiated when we undertake given tasks. The present scientific model doesn't coordinate insightfully with spiritual dimension of life. We're just the action of carbon and proteins; proteins are made of amino acids, which are the building blocks of life. When amino acids and other molecules such as salt and water are mixed, the soup responsible for creating life happens.

Life is composed of lifeless molecules, ever since a molecule began to replicate itself from the raw materials of nature. Dr. Stephen Hawkins says that we are a wonderful biological machine produced through biological evolution. Evolution is a progression that is powerful enough to produce new species from previous species, as the strongest of them all will survive a process called "the survival of the fittest." In the long run, the strongest will morph into other species and that is how life began. Dr. Hawkins continues to explain that life is a process of chain reaction inside a wonderful biological machine, which can carry on indefinitely if some grave disaster does not occur. DNA can replicate itself, and amino acids and other molecules can simply assemble themselves. Dr. Hawkins and others like him explain that we live a while and then die. And the universe? It too has no purpose and no meaning. It is all planned and worked out with no need for spirit. The irony here is—planned by whom, if it has already been laid out?

One should respect the scientific analogy that Dr. Hawkins is adhering to, but in the meanwhile, do not forget that he is only indicating a viable mechanical process taking place in nature that is exhausted of any dynamic life force, which does not explain or question the impetus behind the, as he calls it, "wonderful biological machine." Let's assume that life began about four billion years ago, starting with a single cell that replicated itself and became what we currently are through the intricate process of evolution. Then the question is, how could their claim ever be validated if the precise raw materials and the specific environmental conditions (which could have been comprised of millions, if not billions, of variables) had not been present? I am certain life did not originate in a bubble.

How could such evolutionary advancement ever take place in the absence of a very potent and intelligent energy source—theoretically occurring without a sacred spirit or a ubiquitous soul? If it did, then seeing a dead man walking in a science fiction movie should not raise any eyebrows, as it would be considered as fact. Overwhelming scientific discoveries are readily available that attest to a cosmic energy that is clearly shown in an infinite number of species, making life in its entirety possible. I am afraid Dr. Hawking attributes the cause of such astonishing animated energy to the force of gravity, which he believes is responsible for all there is. Then again, we can only wish it was that easy to extrapolate a definitive conclusion regarding an unanimated thing representing vigorous life-bearing reality. This should alert us not to expand on symbolic lab experiments by stretching them into authenticated fact, because for such a puzzling and complexly intelligent process as the origin of life, such a hardy phenomenon of infinite intricacies is clearly beyond anyone's imagination to empirically determine. Dr. Hawkins' findings should be delivered as hypothesis with no further proof other than speculation.

A new "theory of everything" demands an insightfully convincing theory rather than a materialistic model that denies the tutelage of an enigmatic soul. This can only denote unripe knowledge yet callous wisdom in acknowledging truth as a vehicle by means of neuroscience; I am afraid it is constrained only to lab work as it tries to decode the material brain, and therefore distracted from realizing the intricacy of the definitive human mind and transcendent soul. Limited scientific views have deselected the soul as an object of human belief, and reduced it to a psychological idea that forms our cognition of the perceptible natural world. Such a theory holds that the delivery of "life" and "death" is no more than the common notion of "biological life" and "biological death." The active assumption is simply that the laws of chemistry, physics, and all that exist are just dust orbiting the core of the universe. This assumption unreasonably perceives the energy-driven cosmos as lifeless, which is contrary to the colloquial scientific view which states that everything is purposefully programed to collectively fulfill its destiny. Nature and biocentric agendas are energy-driven and cooperatively spearheaded to fulfill this destiny. Because the physical world is observed through our limited senses, our present worldview contains serious flaws; this should remind us of the great spiritual thinkers and philosophers who tirelessly sought the link between the human mind and the conscious universe. Some of them arrived at a much more convincing outcome than what science has to say.

It is no longer dubious that consciousness is the core that animates life, and helps to make sense of our views of the reality of the cosmos. Even though the contemporary scientific paradigm is based on the credence that the world has an objective observer-independent existence; real trials suggest the antithesis. A great number think life is just the activity of atoms and particles that spin around for a while and then dissipate into nothingness, but if we add life to the equation we can elaborate on some of the major puzzles of science, including the uncertainty principle, ultimately enhance the understanding of the laws that shape our universe.

Let's contemplate the famous "double-slit experiment," and the phenomenon of the observer effect. When one watches a particle enter through the slits, it maneuvers like a bullet, passing through one slit or the other. However, when no one observes the particle, it exhibits the action of a wave and can pass through both slits simultaneously. Similar experiments tell us that undetected particles exist only as "waves of probability," as the great Nobel laureate Max Born proved in 1926. They're statistical predictions—nothing but a likely consequence. Until observed, they have no real existence. Only when the mind sets the framework in place can they be thought of as having duration or a position in space. Experiments make it unavoidably clear that even mere knowledge in the experimenter's mind is good enough to flip-flop possibility to reality. Many scientists believe that observer-dependent behavior applies not only in the sub-atomic world, but that "quantum strange" also happens in the human-scale world.

When referencing whether humans and other living creatures actually have souls, Kant, over two hundred years ago, pointed out: "Everything we experience—including all the colors, sensations and objects we perceive— is nothing but representations in our mind. Space and time are simply the mind's tools for putting it all together." Will Durant wrote, "The hope of another life gives us courage to meet our own death, and to bear with the death of our loved ones; we are twice armed if we fight with faith." We should be reminded that the human mind and soul are not visible and materially oriented, but the effects are known and can be experienced. For example, living a worthy life is not possible without having a sound mind, since our mind is also believed to be a derivative of our physical brain. If this is the case, why should the human soul that is irrefutably integrated with our powerful emotions and feelings be any different from a non-visible mind? Why are scientists and other scholarly-minded individuals not able to identify the real substance behind human thoughts, the essence of our ideas and where they come from? They bombard us every second, yet no one has an inkling how ideas are manufactured or formed and what are they made of.

How can the human soul, which scientists probably expect to relate to atoms, protons, neutron and electrons or any kind of matter, make any sense? Perhaps they expect to find it in the laboratory. I believe there should not be any ambiguity in the search for understanding the human soul, because we need to ask: who or what is it that cries when unhappy and pressured? What and who is it that laughs and feels joy when happy and vibrant? What and who is it that hopes and desires? What or who is it that gets nervous, panics, becomes frightened and desperately seeks to be free, is in search of progress, and diligently tries to be somebody? What or who acts heartened and captivatingly displays courage for the right reasons? It becomes sad when faces injustice; it feels pity and becomes depressed when others are in need of food and shelter. It feels stranded, frustrated and lost when deprived of love, like a dead man walking. It envies, is rejuvenated when in love, and wants to conquer the world. It jumps to its death to save an innocent life. It hates to be alone and can get alarmingly belligerent and dangerous. It acts manic and behaves insanely; it acts wise, it seeks logic, it acts greedy, it acts cool, it has purpose, it seeks happiness, It attracts love and repulses fear, adores being praised and seeks human rights and freedom. It reasons, it chooses, it gets curious, it is judgmental, it has willpower; it manifests consciousness, it conveys intelligence and constitutes the strongest forces to challenge nature. It perseveres and is adamant to breed; it wants to ensure the life continuum for others to come and the next generation to be. It is like being hypnotized and programmed without our consent. It seems to be on autopilot as it is pre-programed, and predestined.

It might sound far-fetched, but we should keep digging until one day humanity can perhaps catch up with its soul-searching ideas, where spiritual endeavors and undertakings are prioritized ahead of our quest for materialism and pride. Part of the problem is that we are putting up with so many egregious disparities that take our very soul hostage while we try just to survive that it leaves no time for any soul-searching. Our spirit belongs to higher dimensions; we should realize this and let it connect to the infinite power of the universe, where it belongs.

It is only then that humanity can reach its true essence. It is not an easy task because our mind and spirit are caged, fettered to fit the present standard of living and caught in the web of uncertainty and materialism. It sure makes it difficult to quench our thirst, seeking true love and letting our soul evolve into aesthetic living to objectify happiness and enrich the way we live. This can potentiate the image of God in man and propel humanity toward reaching higher realms, if only given a chance.

Essay 12
A Déjà vu.

A Déjà vu: is defined as the illusion of remembering scenes and events when experienced for the first time, a feeling that one has seen or heard something gratifying before, something overly or unpleasantly familiar, same old, same old. Or an anecdote: which means an uncontrolled or poorly documented observation or experience.

The above should remind us of the same redundant mistakes we hatch in making crucial decisions since so many people act blindly. Because they relate to conventional wisdom that is hindered by pride and outdated through cultural tendencies, and prone to hazards outcome that are intentionally or unknowingly ignored.

The magnitude of damages done is sometimes irreparable and can affect us for a long time. But still delusional and not able to assess the real dilemmas, or perhaps deficient in realizing the cause of the actual problem.

Allow me to be specific and more in tune with the recent bloody events and the so called revolutions that took place in many Middle East and African countries. As the masses of innocent people were maimed, slaughtered, imprisoned and tortured with no merci, which of-course these revolting nations were left with no availability to a dynamic change for restoring a viable solution for democracy or in achieving any freedom at all.

It seems that we are purposely overlooking pattern recognition and in denial of seeing the reality of vital factors that play significant role in crucial matters when dealing with dictatorial governments and their nations. Our exposure effect, meaning our inclination to more favorably rated things or believes with which we are more familiar and like to acquaint with, can lead us away from the reality of what is actually happening, which then plenty of people act biased and stray from the truth. There are many instances of those who fought for democracy, liberty and freedom but when placed in power they done grave harms if not worse than the meanest of them all. The problem is mitigated when people avoid rendering the absolute power in one's hand and relinquish puissance to a national council to act as a legislative body, or nominating a government of the republic.

This wicket redundancy occurs despite heavy prices paid and sacrifices made by the masses, it can only be recalled as a déjà vu and not a lesson learned; because we must exercise the plasticity to face such vital task scientifically and appropriately, since a viable transformation of power calls for a nation to be knowledgeable and deem to have learned and deciphered lessons from the past.

It is crucial to truly understand the exclusive social order, and to comprehend the psychological, economical, and political pattern in a given society, to further respect the influence of the fundamental cultural and traditional forces imposed on it.

In the mean-while, it is also necessary to act brave and courage's enough to incrementally introduce new and progressive ideas wisely, where up-to-date moves is evaluated with reason, since they need to be compatible with masses liking, and if so, then in nudging people to collaborate with modern agendas. It is further vital to encourage the potentiality for dynamic changes and to gradually calibrate and modify outdated rules until the overall society is ripe and ready for a leap of action in substantiating radical social movement, and perhaps to be blessed with a new horizon.

This is whole procedure can burst into an ugly upheaval, hence it is extremely case sensitive which demands expert and professional leadership, a superb management and an instrumental master mind that could factor in the nation's entire risk taking; as they need to observe and recognize all the weak and strong points where they should not blunder, or to foozle. Because grave endeavor as such forces people to take risk and go beyond their means, and sometimes without any significant back-up.

What we tend to forget there are powerful governments that work in concert to vehemently protect trillion and trillions of dollars invested globally, which must accrue more capital every second beneficial to the corporate class, the elites and the aristocrats, the king and the queens of our time, as they are adamant to keep the status quo.

They very cleverly define freedom and democracy to serve them well, that should remind us of what was commonly said by the Athenians which they invented democracy, but if so, it was a democracy for the rich. And since the opulent represent themselves as the guardian of liberty and the advocate of human rights, where ironically under their influence millions of innocent people and the poor literally become trampled, or lose their precious lives without moral turpitude or any legal repercussion for the mighty culprits. The privilege class believe if there are changes to be made it needs to serve their interest, so that it can pass their approval and to permit a green light, before any meaningful law is materialized.

We ought to know the transnational corporation's immediate interest is at stake, as we have reached a globalization phase in our economy where zillions of funds and enormous effort and energy is spent in international investments. Not to exclude outsourcing of productive forces, including capital, new technologies, updated machineries, raw material, skillful labor, etc. Which has become the norms, and therefore any prospect for comprising a new government elsewhere must guaranty and satisfy these powerful entities, and the custodian of wealth and their interest. And no matter how valid the referendums and or elected officials are favored by their populace natives, they will be damned if behave otherwise, and not to comply.

Essay 13
Freedom and Democracy

Freedom is a predominant concept that the overall majority of nations seek and desire to have, especially developing and dictatorial countries. Understanding that the notion of freedom is not an easy task and is an inherently complicated matter should remind us of the expression, "be careful what you wish for." Freedom is a sacred word that needs to be understood and practiced with the utmost care and intelligence, because when freedom is abused it impacts us all, as the dire effects will be felt both individually and socially.

Yes, to define the word freedom is to say that you, I, he and she are free to exercise what each of us wish to do. Futurist Jacque Fresco warns, "Democracy is a con game. It's a word invented to placate people to make them accept a given institution. All institutions sing, 'We are free.' The minute you hear 'freedom' and 'democracy', watch out... because in a truly free nation, no one has to tell you you're free." This statement comes from a rational mind, clearly compounded with wise and virtuous character—rare to find these days. Such consideration takes due diligence, perseveration, and tons of constructive work. Knowing there is this unquenchable thirst for self-pampering and need for bodily joy demands openness of mind and sacrifice to overcome, ultimately leading to a practical and efficacious realm of living.

The above referenced matter of wisdom needs to produce desirable, high-caliber personalities with excellent character. These individuals must be invested in professionally and operate with care in order to assist the destitute and the deprived in a timely fashion. It also requires deep pockets—being financially set, so to speak—as well as experience and an accommodative attitude. It takes expertise and tenacity to act as both a role model and a benefactor, influencing others consistent with one's good conscience.

Remember, in free countries you are on your own, and you are perhaps free to do as you wish. You should know, however, that when you do well, your education, talents, and skills are leveraged to conform to what the system is designed for and wants from you. This means walking those cultural and societal guidelines for a successful, and a prosperous life. Then, not only you but perhaps also those around you will benefit society and the system tremendously. An innovative, motivated individual should have the passion to take advantage of the boundless opportunities that are offered, which if positively applied, can become extremely fruitful. The system immediately recognizes a potentially talented mind and does not hesitate to promote it, making one a productive member of society who will be in high demand and rewarded with gold. In this scenario, one reaches his or her dreams, and has accesses to a financial heaven. You are to be promoted and acknowledged as an entrepreneur or successful business person, much like millions of others having similar goals. These individuals are the building blocks of a capitalist system, and are definitely required in a free and vigorous society. We could say it is a win-win situation, since not only you but also the system and society can flourish when acting in harmony.

You ought to keep in mind, however, that God forbid you are directed at will or premeditate causing ill to another, or do wrong by your own choosing. In this case the system certainly wins since you are to be punished harshly with huge fines and confinement, depending on the degree of your wrongdoing. It is only fair to say that in a capitalist system that promotes a stratified society, there must be people available to do menial and horrifying jobs. They are not compensated enough, or even paid any attention to. I categorize these individuals as "faceless people" who must do the dirty jobs to survive, and often have to live with the consequences of an inferiority complex since so many are not able to fulfill what they crave and wish for. Unfortunately this state is sometimes prolonged to last their entire life, which is certainly so sad for those who are not able to reach their dreams. We should bear in mind that when someone is in violation of a free society's systemic code of ethics and what it stands for, the entire society is negatively affected.

One needs to strive toward becoming educated, to seek marketable skills and a professional vocation of some sort that is in high demand and prestigious enough to win one gold and avoid being an outcast. It is a system that brings you goodness and treasure on a silver platter only if you are awakened to its cultural and societal demands; you are then seen as a good candidate to serve the system's tasks. Remember the system always wins, no matter if an individual loses or thrives. A culprit will carry a heavy burden and is penalized for doing wrong; in other words, for not acting as expected.

It is crucial not to get arrogant and/or lured into believing it is a free country and that you can perhaps do what you want with impunity. When one is mischievous and does wrong, society is negatively impacted. The culprit is punished accordingly and hopefully within due process of the law, but the system wins regardless. It would be admirable if the system would manifest itself in productive ways to halt crime by educating and providing meaningful training, rather than being financially motivated and remaining stoic about such vital deeds when encouraging freedom and democracy. Either way there must be a balance in exercising freedom and in acting democratic. Plato said, "Dictatorship naturally arises out of democracy, and the most aggravated form of tyranny and slavery out of the most extreme liberty." When a system is adamant to promote a free society and to unleash democracy, there must exist boundless professional counselors and quality social services to help those in need of mental and behavioral assistance transition to a civilized and rational-minded society.

I believe it is difficult to implement true democracy when people are famished. The disease of hunger must be cured to lessen rampant crimes and to remedy the ills of criminals. Let me be explicit: there is no ambiguity about freedom and the need for education, as well as value-added training with emphasis on the mind and spiritual development. These must go hand in hand when you operate in a free society. The society needs to see its potential deficiencies, and should be able to absorb the seeds of freedom in its fertile ground. This requires irrigation, proper sun, nutrients and care to mature into a fruitful tree. Priorities should be given to those that earnestly believe in acting as true human beings with good conscience. If not, rest assured that society's beastly side shall prevail, leading ultimately to corruption and destruction. So we must ask ourselves this question: God endowed humanity with the miracles of brain and mind. Why can we not, as a society, manifest and make good our individual intelligence, positive emotions, good will and constructive actions to benefit society?

Jawaharlal Nehru, former Prime Minister of India, expresses it this way, "Democracy is good. I say this because other systems are worse." We are forced to accept democracy. It has its good points and also bad, but merely saying that democracy will solve all our problems is utterly wrong. Problems are solved by intelligence and hard work. Thomas Jefferson said, "When the government fears the people there is liberty. When the people fear the government there is tyranny." I say again that society must be potentiated and act upon its collective savviness, being able to distinguish between what is right and what is wrong and to behave accordingly. If not, we are better off tolerating a dictatorial regime to prevent a blood bath on a larger scale.

We should also be reminded that the more educated, civilized and also opulent the nation, the more democracy is practical and freedom should make sense We also need to bear in mind that even the wisest nation can act barbaric when slapped with hunger and insecurity. In this case, fear and anxiety replaces civility of mind and manner and this can threaten democracy and peace. Either way, humanity must push for meaningful freedom and constructive democracy. Noam Chomsky puts it this way: "In this possibly terminal phase of human existence, democracy and freedom are more than just ideals to be valued-they may be essential to survival." The bottom line: before any nation can truly capitalize on freedom and democracy, it is vital to know that the human species by nature encapsulates the common good, despite due diligence efforts to psychologically undermine and alienate people to behave otherwise. Collectivism and cooperation is discouraged, since anyone or any group not belonging to a specific race or league is demonized due to the prevalence of bigotry.

It is not a natural human impulse to behave in a divided and segregated manner. Human beings are group animals that can dynamically flourish with teamwork—and that is exactly why we have evolved, and are able, so far, to survive modern times. There would be serious flaws and a conflict of interest in our literal implementation of freedom and democracy without sincere belief inclusive to the acceptance of everyone, regardless of race, nationality, religion, gender, traits or any trend of thought which one might have. Let's not forget that freedom and democracy demand open-mindedness, courage, compassion, tolerance, sacrifice, and true respect for human rights. Mankind should feel at home where one should happily belong.

About the Author

Dr. Feridoun Shawn Shahmoradian showed an avid interest in learning about other cultures from a very young age. Shawn's love for people as well as his need to quench a thirst for learning about others' ways of life inspired him to travel extensively to many parts of the world, including the Middle East, Persia, Turkey (Istanbul, Ankara), Europe, West Africa, and North America. His travels have rewarded him with an invaluable wealth of knowledge and experience, allowing him to acquire realistic views in the context of diversified cultural, philosophical, social, political, economic, and psychological endeavors.

Dr. Shawn attended many spiritual and callisthenic seminars in different parts of the world, including Morocco (Rabat, Marrakech city, Fes, and Casablanca), Oslo, Paris, Amsterdam, Dublin (Ireland), Toronto (Canada) and Monroe (California), San Diego (California), New Jersey, Orlando (Florida), Dallas, Houston, and Galveston (Texas) in the United Sates of America. He then visited New York, Washington, Las Vegas, San Antonio, Austin, El Paso, Corpus Christi, Texas, New Orleans, Miami Beach, Mexico (Mexico City, Cancun, Cozumel), and Bahamas.

At the age of seventeen, Shawn attended Crawley College in Crawley, England, for about three consecutive years and also attended boarding school at Birchington-on-Sea. He visited London several times, resided at Brighton for a while, and visited Hastings, Canterbury, and Sheffield. Dr. Shawn then travelled to Fresno and San Francisco, California, and went to Lake Tahoe, Nevada, to teach.

Dr. Shawn then left to study at Stockton College in Stockton, California, for two full years, taking philosophy and other social science courses. He then transferred to Galveston Texas College for one more year. A couple years later, he received his electronic engineering degree from Texas Southern University in Houston, Texas. He furthered his studies at Texas A & M and received his master's degree in economics. His love for social science motivated him to attend the University of Texas at Dallas in Dallas, Texas, and there he obtained a master's degree in public affairs.

Dr. Shawn's obsession with sports and a relentless pursuit for excellence in the art of self-defense that he pursued while facing insurmountable challenges over many years makes him a true embodiment of wisdom and strength. After extensive and thorough research in a variety of arts, Dr. Shawn finally created the Pang-Fang system, a very unique and practical system approved and highly recommended by authorities in the field of self-defense.

Dr. Shawn holds a ninth-degree black belt in hapkido, a Korean martial art, and holds a tenth-degree black belt in the Pang-Fang system. He is acknowledged as a prominent figure and as a holder of a nonconventional doctorate degree in sports and the art of self-defense. Dr. Shawn is the author of the book Mind Fighter and the book of The Anatomy of Wake-Up Calls Volume 1.

Printed in the United States
By Bookmasters